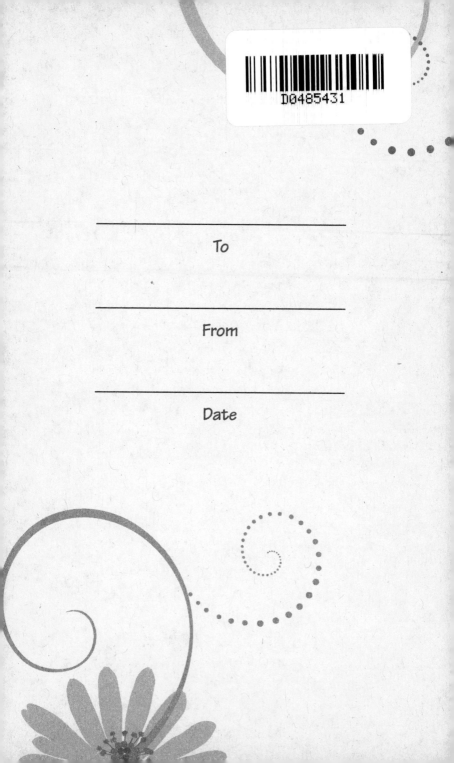

_____

To

_____

From

_____

Date

"*Praying for Your Future Husband* shows young women how to love and serve the man they will marry—even before meeting him! A practical and encouraging book that helps girls invest in their future marriages right now."

—LESLIE LUDY, best-selling author of *When God Writes Your Love Story* and *Authentic Beauty*

"Full of wisdom, vulnerable honesty, and inspiration, *Praying for your Future Husband* is a book every young Christian woman should read. In thinking about the man of their dreams, they'll encounterwho the One and Only wants them to be first—His."

—Lisa T. Bergren, author of *Waterfall, The Busy Mom's Devotional,* and *Life on Planet Mom*

"This book is a must-read for every girl who has even wondered what her future husband will be like. Every page left me wishing I'd had this book when I was still single—or during all the years I mentored boy-crazy teenage girls. Whether you are looking for inspiration, encouragement, or even proof that prayer works, this book is for you. The perfect blend of real-life stories and a how-to manual, *Praying for Your Future Husband* will be an ideal companion from now until the altar."

—SHANNON PRIMICERIO, author of *The Divine Dance, God Called a Girl,* and the TrueLife Bible Studies series

"When I was twelve years old, my husband began praying for me. I did not know that, of course, because I did not yet know him or

God. But later, looking back, I saw how those prayers had miraculously affected my life. Gunn and Goyer are practical, vulnerable, inspirational, and encouraging. I can think of few better gifts for a young lady to offer her future husband than the gift of her prayers, and this book shows how to do it."

—SANDRA BYRD, best-selling author of the London
Confidential series and other books for teens and tweens

"*Praying for Your Future Husband* is packed with wisdom and overflowing with practical insight to encourage the heart of every young woman seeking God's best. The perfect blending of Robin's and Tricia's unique and personal journeys to find their mates, it is filled with wisdom and sound advice from Scripture to spur on your prayer life as you follow your own path. This is a *must*-read for every young woman who desires a road map on the journey of discovering God's heart!"

—PAM STENZEL, MA, author of *Nobody Told Me* and *Sex Has
a Price Tag* and director of Enlighten Communications

"Are you tired of waiting for the right man and convinced that all the good guys are already taken? Want to find the man who will love you and cherish you, having been prepared by the Lord himself? This book is where you begin. Robin and Tricia have taken all the pieces of the "finding true love" puzzle and have assembled a clear picture and a path that make sense and tell the truth about God and His plans for you. Stop worrying, and dive right in. This book shows you each step of the way to a future that God has planned for you and your future husband!"

—AMANDA BENNETT, author of more than ninety books

Praying
for Your
Future Husband

Preparing Your Heart for His

Robin Jones Gunn
and Tricia Goyer

MULTNOMAH
BOOKS

Praying for Your Future Husband
Published by Multnomah Books
12265 Oracle Boulevard, Suite 200
Colorado Springs, Colorado 80921

SPECIAL SALES
Most WaterBrook Multnomah books are available at special quantity discounts when purchased in bulk by corporations, organizations, and special-interest groups. Custom imprinting or excerpting can also be done to fit special needs. For information, please e-mail SpecialMarkets@WaterBrook Multnomah.com or call 1-800-603-7051.

From Robin:

To my daughter, Rachel.
You prayed, you waited, you trusted, and God answered.
Oh how He answered!
Let the happily-forever-after begin!

From Tricia:

To my daughter Leslie.
Like stars in the night sky, there are millions of guys to wish on.
Praying with you to find the one who will make
your dreams come true.
And may you draw closer to the Eternal One as you seek him.

GOD proves to be good to the man
    who passionately waits,
to the woman who diligently seeks.
It's a good thing to quietly hope,
quietly hope for help from GOD.
It's a good thing when you're young
to stick it out through the hard times.
When life is heavy and hard to take,
go off by yourself. Enter the silence.
Bow in prayer. Don't ask questions:
Wait for hope to appear.

—LAMENTATIONS 3:25–29 (MSG)

Contents

An *Extraordinary* Mystery

Robin:

Sometimes, when an idea just won't go away, you need to pay attention to how God is nudging you. That's what happened with this book.

Tricia and I have been friends for almost two decades, and both of us are writers. But our life stories as well as our love stories are radically different. Beyond writing, we do have one interesting commonality: both of us prayed for our future husbands when we were teens. But how did that add up to our writing a book together? Three incidents convinced us we should...

The first moment of inspiration fell on me with a weighty sense of urgency one bright November afternoon. I was in Brazil, standing in front of three hundred teen girls in a school cafeteria. My Christy Miller and Sierra Jensen novels for teens have been translated into Portuguese, and the teachers at this school use the books as part of their curriculum. That meant all the girls had read the books. When my husband and I entered the cafeteria, the girls greeted us with a wave of screams as if we were the real Christy and Todd all grown up and visiting them in Brazil.

To quiet down the screaming girls, I asked the translator to invite them to ask questions. One of the girls raised her hand and popped up from her seat. In Portuguese she asked me what she and her friends should do since the boys in Brazil weren't reading my books.

"What do you mean?" I asked.

She spoke passionately as the translator beside me explained. "She says that, after reading your books, she and her friends are making good decisions. They've given their lives to Christ and now want to stay pure and save themselves for their future husbands. But, you see, the boys of Brazil are not reading these books. They are not making these same decisions. She wants to know what can be done about that."

My heart pounded. Every face in that cafeteria was fixed on me, waiting for an answer. The young woman had just identified a global problem for our present generation of Christian women. I had heard this frustration voiced many times in letters and e-mails I had received from readers over the years. But no one had ever asked me what could be done to change this dilemma of an unbalanced ratio between God-honoring young women and their male contemporaries who were slow to seek God. What could I tell her?

The words that came out of my heart were, "You have work to do, dear God-Lover Girls. You must start praying for your future husband now."

The translator gave her my answer, and a reverent hush fell over the room. Before me was a troop of willing but untrained young women ready to enter the war zone to fight for their young men. But how?

I wished then that I had something more to offer those girls. It's one thing to tell them to pray and another thing to come alongside and show them what that looks like.

The second defining moment came two years later. Tricia and I were at a writers' retreat in California. During the afternoon break, we headed out to the pool. I settled in a lounge chair and wrote notes in my journal for a novel I was working on. Tricia succumbed to the luxurious autumn sunshine and floated off into a deep sleep.

Suddenly she woke up, turned to me, and said, "What?" as if I'd been talking to her while she slept.

I looked at her and spoke an unpremeditated thought. "Tricia, we need to write a book together."

"Okay." She didn't even blink before sinking back into her afternoon lull. A moment later her head rose again. "What are we supposed to write about?"

"I have no idea."

The gentle notion flitted past me as softly as it had fallen on Tricia. We caught the little inspiration the way an artist would reach for a floating feather or a child would bend to pick up a pale blue pebble and tuck it in a pocket.

Over the next year or so we periodically pulled the small inspiration out of our pockets and talked about what we should write. We had lots of ideas, as all creative people do. But the affirmation and direction weren't there. So we waited, and we prayed...

The third moment of inspiration came with such defining clarity we knew what the book was to be about.

Tricia and I were in Montana, preparing to speak at a women's retreat. The night before the retreat we sneaked off to a lodge for some last-minute planning. I entered the lodge first while Tricia parked the car in the snow. A darling little strawberry-blond toddler trotted over to me, put up his arms, and allowed me to scoop him up. His surprised young mom told me his name was Toby, he was eighteen months old, and he was usually not that friendly with strangers. Toby patted my face.

Tricia entered, and Toby's mother froze. She stared at Tricia and in a shaking voice said, "It's you! You're the one who spoke at the luncheon two years ago."

Tricia spoke often at events for teenage girls and women in Montana, so I doubted she would remember this particular young woman from a luncheon two years ago. The mom said, "Do you remember that you talked about being a teen mom and that you prayed God would send you a Christian husband?"

Tricia nodded.

"I did the same thing. I prayed and..." She leaned in closer. "I don't know if you remember my telling you this after the luncheon, but I had just found out I was pregnant."

"I remember," Tricia said.

"I had planned on having an abortion the following week." The young woman gazed at Toby cuddled up in my arms. "But after I heard your story and what you said about how God answered your prayers, I cancelled the appointment for the abortion, and I prayed for a husband, just like you did."

Her smile widened, and tears formed in her eyes as she told Tricia, "I always wanted to see you again so I could tell you that God answered my prayers. He brought an amazing Christian guy into my life. He loves me, and he loves my son. We've been married for almost a year. When I think about what my life would be like right now if I hadn't heard your story and done what you said…"

By then we were all hugging and crying and hugging some more. Toby climbed into Tricia's arms and received her cuddles and kisses. We couldn't stop crying. It was such a beautiful moment. The room seemed full of light and hope.

After Toby and his mama went their way, Tricia and I sat together in stunned silence. We both knew this was it—this was the theme of the book we needed to write together: praying for your future husband. We also knew we were the two unlikely novelists being invited to pour our hearts into this project. And so we did.

As we wrote, what tumbled from our hearts surprised us. We didn't compose a handbook on techniques or formulas for effective prayer. Through the ages many wonderful such books have been written. Instead, what we saw forming, as we met together to pray and write, was a book anchored with true stories about what happens when women pray for their future husbands and the ways God answers those prayers.

Both of us agreed to tell our own stories on these pages. This took some courage. Dozens of other women gave us permission to tell portions of their stories as well—how they prayed, how God chose to answer, and how their lives changed in the process. This took courage for them as well. We pulled from our Bibles and journals favorite scriptures and excerpts. These quotes worked perfectly to lace the chapters together.

As the book took shape, we discovered that prayer is an extraordinary mystery.

This sacred privilege of communicating with our Heavenly Father is more than a cozy, open invitation to come to Him anytime, anywhere. Even though His ears are open to the cries of His children 24/7, prayer is more than that. Prayer is also an act of obedience. We are exhorted to pray for others and to pray without ceasing.

Neither Tricia nor I pretend to have prayer all figured out. What we do know is that God hears. He sees. He knows us. He cares more than we can ever comprehend. And most important of all, God answers prayer.

Perhaps you've noticed that oftentimes the way God answers prayers isn't what we expect. We look back years later and see that what God did was oh so much better than what we first envisioned when we sent our heartfelt requests heavenward. He created us, and He desires the best for us. God always gives His best to those who leave the outcomes with Him.

Another even more amazing mystery is that when we pray for someone else, we change. All of us were made both to give love and to receive love. When your heart connects through prayer to the One who is the source of true love, you'll find that praying for your future husband will wondrously result in your heart being changed. And when your heart is changed, your life is transformed.

What sort of changes will God bring about in the life of your future husband as a result of your praying for him now? We don't know.

As you pray for him, what sort of changes will God initiate in your heart? We don't know that either.

But we do know there's only one way to find out…

2

Pray

for

His Heart

My heart has heard you say,
"Come and talk with me."
And my heart responds,
"Lord, I am coming."
—Psalm 27:8 (nlt)

Robin:

Here's a little secret about true love: it begins in the heart.

"Yes, yes, we all know that," you say. Ever since you received your first red, heart-shaped valentine, you've associated the heart as the place where love appears, sets up camp, and lights a warming fire. The heart is where lasting relationships begin and are kept aflame.

Anyone who has suffered from a broken heart knows that the heart is also the vulnerable place where relationships can be snuffed out. The smoke and scent of smoldering ashes can cloud your spirit and blur your vision for a long time.

I've always thought of the heart as being like a garden. Whatever is planted there will eventually grow if it is nurtured. The fruit of that garden will be evidenced in a person's words and actions. Just as God placed the first man and woman in a garden and met with them there in the cool of the evening, God still comes walking in the garden of our hearts and calls out to us, as He did to Adam and Eve, asking, "Where are you?"

How do we respond to that call? Adam and Eve were honest after they realized they had disobeyed God, and they responded with, "We were afraid, and so we hid."

The place to start praying for your future husband is in the garden of his heart. What do you want to be growing there when you meet him? Is he hiding from God now? How about you? Have you come out of hiding?

I came out of hiding when I was thirteen years old. I was at summer camp, and the speaker said something that really got to me. "God doesn't have any grandchildren," he said. "Just because your parents are Christians, doesn't make you a Christian."

I had been going to church my whole life, and I assumed I was a Christian by association or membership or something my parents had done. The speaker invited us to stay in the chapel after the evening meeting if we wanted to talk with the counselors about how we could have a relationship with Christ.

My objective all week had, in fact, been to start a new relationship. But the relationship I wanted was with Bill Vander-land. I wanted him to become my boyfriend. Starting a forever relationship with the Lord hadn't appeared anywhere on my wish list when I arrived at Taquitz Pines with my girlfriends from church.

One of my friends, Candi, got a boy interested in her the very first night at the campfire. By Wednesday she and Dale were holding hands under the picnic table at craft time. On Thursday night they kissed behind the chapel. By Friday after-noon Dale asked Candi to be his girlfriend, and all the rest of us girls in cabin four were in awe. How did she do that? We wished we could be just like Candi. Every one of us longed to be desired and sought after. We wanted to be loved.

As far as Bill becoming my boyfriend that week, well, that just wasn't happening. I did manage to catch his attention be-fore camp ended, though. At dinner on Friday night, I sat at the table behind his and stared at the back of his head through the entire meal. Inwardly I whispered, *Come on. Turn around. Look at me. Notice me. Talk to me.*

The moment of opportunity came. One of my cabin mates said something silly, and I burst out laughing extra loud. I mean, really-extra-about-to-snort-and-wheeze loud.

It worked! Bill turned around. He looked at me! And that was it. The beginning and end of my camp romance.

Or was it?

While Candi and Dale sneaked off behind the Ping-Pong room after the meeting on Friday night, I stayed to talk to my counselor. She told me that God had been pursuing me since the day I was born and that He longed to have a restored relationship with me, with all of us.

I knew how it felt to want to have a relationship with Bill and end up being ignored. I wondered if that's how God felt about me. I knew that I hid from Him whenever I did something wrong. Just like Adam and Eve, I tried to cover up and not be found out.

"That's why we need Jesus," my counselor explained. "His death and resurrection made a way for us to enter into a forever relationship with our Heavenly Father."

I'm sure I had heard a lot of the things she was saying during my years of going to church, but that night it all made sense. The invitation to enter into an open relationship with God was extended to me at the heart level, and I believed.

While Candi and Dale were exchanging kisses and promises behind the Ping-Pong room, I bowed my head beside my camp counselor and opened the gate to the garden of my heart. I invited Jesus to come in and to clean things up, to plant new thoughts, hopes, and dreams in the freshly turned soil.

The life-altering prayer I whispered that night went something like this: *Lord, please forgive me for everything I've done that has made You sad. I surrender my life to You. Please come into my heart. I want to live the life You dreamed up when You created me. Amen.*

That night a deep longing inside of me was filled. Not with a camp boyfriend but with the presence of the One who promised never to leave me or abandon me.

On the bus ride home from camp, I sat behind Candi and Dale. I watched them cuddle up and wished I were going home with a boyfriend too. I thought about what I had prayed the night before. Did I really mean it when I said I wanted to live the life God had planned for me? What if His plan meant I wouldn't have a boyfriend anytime soon? Or worse, what if God didn't intend for me to marry?

Suddenly the idea of surrendering my life to God's will seemed quite dangerous.

And to be honest, trusting God, surrendering my life to Him, and being in a forever relationship with Jesus has indeed been dangerous. He is in control. Not me. Crazy things have happened over the years. But living each day with Christ has also been breathtaking and beautiful and way, way beyond my wildest hopes. I know now that I wouldn't want to live any other life than the one God dreamed up when He created me.

During my early high school years, when I started to think about the kind of guy I might marry someday, I knew he had to be a Christian too. To be in a life-partner relationship with someone who didn't follow Christ would feel as if we were unequally yoked, as the apostle Paul wrote about in 2 Corinthians 6:14. I wanted my husband to have the same close connection with God because I knew that would make us even closer as a couple.

I often prayed, *God, if You have a guy for me to marry someday, then I pray that he will become a Christian if he isn't one already.*

What I didn't realize was that praying for my future husband to have a heart-to-heart relationship with God was only the beginning. God had more expansive plans for my prayers, plans that would prepare *my* heart as I prayed for *his*.

Tricia's early teen years were different from mine, but as you'll see before this book ends, God had His hand on her life all the way through, just as He has His hand on your life and your future husband's life. He has amazing plans for each of us.

> "For I know the plans I have for you," declares the
> LORD, "plans to prosper you and not to harm you,
> plans to give you hope and a future. Then you will
> call on me and come and pray to me, and I will listen
> to you."
> —Jeremiah 29:11–12 (NIV)

Tricia:

I started to dream about my future husband earlier than Robin did. My dreaming began when I was ten years old. I knew I wanted to be married and live in a little house with six children, two dogs, and one cat. I never knew my biological dad growing up. My mom and stepdad had separated more than once, and things weren't looking good. I was determined to marry the right man and to stay in love with him the rest of my life.

When I met Steven, I was only thirteen, but I was certain he was The One.

A week later Steven's sister, Tracey, invited me over to their house. Tracey and I took our sodas on the back porch and watched Steven shoot arrows at targets he had set up in the backyard.

"Do you want to try?" Steven asked.

The bow was heavier than I thought. I picked up an arrow and positioned it.

I tried to pull back on the bowstring, but it wouldn't budge.

"Here, let me help you with that." Steven stood behind me and wrapped his arms around mine. I could feel his chest on my back. His breath was warm on my cheek. His left hand covered mine as I gripped the bow. Two fingers of his right hand wrapped around the strings right above mine, and he helped to pull it back.

"On the count of three, release," he whispered. "One, two, three."

The arrow released from the bow and sailed through the air. It hit in the second ring of the target.

"Good hit!" Tracey called out.

We practiced a few more shots, and then Tracey was called inside to set the table for dinner.

"Come on." Steven set the bow on a bale of hay. "I want to talk to you about something."

I followed him to the enclosed back porch. As I leaned against the wall, his eyes were on me. I felt hot all over, and my knees trembled. I hoped they would hold me up, especially when Steven stepped closer. I wasn't sure they would.

"My sister says you like me."

"She said that?"

He laughed. "Do you?"

I shrugged, hoping not to look too desperate. "Yeah."

"Good." He approached, placing his hand on the wall behind my shoulder. "Because I like you too."

This moment felt like everything I'd waited for. For as long as I could remember, I had wondered if, like Cinderella, I would someday have my own Prince Charming. As I gazed into Steven's beautiful blue eyes, I could imagine us being together forever, dating through high school, getting married right after college.

He smiled and leaned closer. His fingertips brushed my cheeks. Steven's eyes were on mine, and his lips were only inches away.

I held my breath and accepted my first kiss. My first prayer for my future husband came quickly after that. *Please, God, make Steven always love me as much as I love him.*

I was certain what I prayed was the right sort of thing to ask God—to request that He make everything work out the way I wanted it to. But there was a problem: I wasn't a Christian, and I didn't understand how prayer worked. I didn't yet understand about the heart connection that needed to be in place between God and me and between God and my future husband.

Here's what I now know about what prayer is and what it isn't.

What Prayer Is	What Prayer Isn't
Entering into a conversation with God	Viewing God as a grantor of our wishes
Seeking God's direction with choices	Asking God for a stamp of approval on decisions
Humbling ourselves before Almighty God	Demanding our rights

> The whole meaning of prayer is that we may know God.
>
> —OSWALD CHAMBERS

WHAT ABOUT YOU?

How close is your relationship with God?

Our Heavenly Father is holy and perfect. We are frail and flawed. God's Word has made it clear that the only way for us to experience a heart-to-heart relationship with God is through His Son, Jesus.

The amazing good news in all this is that Jesus wants a relationship with us more than we can imagine. The perfect time to open the gate to the garden of your heart is today. Now. This very moment. The exact words you pray don't matter as much as the attitude of your heart. You are speaking with Almighty God, the Creator of the universe. He made you. He knows you.

Since the day you were born, He has desired that you would come out of hiding.

> Call to me, and I will answer you. I will tell you
> great and mysterious things that you do not know.
> —Jeremiah 33:3 (God's Word)

HOW DO I BEGIN TO PRAY FOR MY FUTURE HUSBAND'S HEART?

- You begin by entering into a heart-to-heart relationship with God yourself.
- Pray that your future husband will become a Christian.
- Pray that he will read God's Word and that it will transform his heart.
- Pray that the Lord will clear any of the obstacles in the path that are keeping him from coming to Christ.
- Pray that God will send someone to tell him the good news of salvation.
- Pray that God will prepare his heart to hear and respond to God's call.

SHE PRAYED...GOD ANSWERED

When I was eighteen, I was praying for my future husband more than usual. A year later we met, and I found out that during the time I had been praying intensely for him, he was trying to determine what he was going to do with his life. He'd just come back from another state where he'd been a television cameraman for a network. I'd like to think my prayers played a part in God directing him on a path that would lead him to me. —Gena

Dear Robin, for many years I've wanted to tell you what happened since the days when you were my Sunday school teacher. When I met my husband, he wasn't a believer. After we had been together a couple of years, he asked me to marry him. At that moment I had to grow up. You see, I made a promise to God and to you, my seventh-grade Sunday school teacher, that I wouldn't get married "unequally yoked." You had us make a list of "Boyfriend/Husband Character Prerequisites," and on the top of that list was that our mate was to be a believer and follower of Jesus.

I told Olivier I couldn't marry him. He was a Frenchman from a secular Jewish family that had survived the Holocaust. I was a California girl who grew up in a Christian family and at a church where the Bible was the final authority in all of life.

I prayed all the time for Olivier. I continually encouraged him to read the Bible and study the Messianic prophecies, which he did for a short while, to no avail. Eventually I gave him a copy of *The Late Great Planet Earth* by Hal Lindsey. It was through God's Word, found in that book, that Olivier came to the realization that he needed Yeshua in his life. Soon after that, I had the privilege of leading Olivier to his Messiah, Yeshua. He asked me again to marry him, and this time I said yes.

We've been married for twenty-seven years and have experienced God's extreme blessings as we have spent our lives "equally yoked," taking the message of the Messiah to the Jewish people. —Ellen

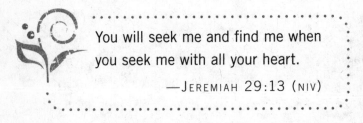

You will seek me and find me when you seek me with all your heart.
—JEREMIAH 29:13 (NIV)

BEFORE YOU BEGIN PRAYING FOR YOUR FUTURE HUSBAND, CONSIDER THIS

In John 15, Jesus explained to His disciples how this asking and receiving from our Heavenly Father worked. As a matter of fact, the example He gave is in garden terms. Jesus said, "I am the true grapevine, and my Father is the gardener" (verse 1, NLT). He then told us where we fit into this picture: "I am the vine; you are the branches. Those who remain in me, and I in them, will produce much fruit. For apart from me you can do nothing" (verse 5, NLT).

Praying isn't an exercise in whimsically sending off a wish into the clouds. Nor is it an audience with the king during which we stand as beggars with a list of pleas. When we enter into a forever relationship with Christ, God adopts us into His family. We are His children. You become a daughter of the King of this universe. Just as Jesus described, you are a branch, connected to the vine. His Spirit flows through you.

Now consider this. In verses 7–8 Jesus said, "If you abide in Me, and My words abide in you, you will ask what you desire, and it shall be done for you. By this My Father is glorified, that you bear much fruit; so you will be My disciples" (NKJV).

TRUE LOVE BEGINS IN THE HEART

The best place for you to begin praying for your future husband is in the garden of your heart. Become God's daughter and see yourself as a branch connected to Jesus, who is the true vine. Abide in Him. Read your Bible so that His words of truth will abide in you. Then, as a trusting daughter, tell your Heavenly Father what you desire.

> Delight yourself in the LORD;
> And He will give you the desires of your heart.
> —Psalm 37:4 (NASB)

A PRAYER FOR MY FUTURE HUSBAND

Father God, I pray that if my future husband doesn't already know You, You will bring him into Your forever kingdom. I pray that my future husband will seek You and find You. I pray that he will seek You with all his heart. I pray that Your Holy Spirit will draw him to You and that his heart will be softened and ready to surrender to You.

So many things in this world draw us away from You. I pray that my future husband will not be distracted from the truth. May he discover that You are the Lover of his soul and that his most important relationship is the one he has with You. I pray that no matter what his friends are doing, he will turn to You and that You will be the most important person in his life.

I ask this in Jesus' name, amen.

A Prayer for Me

Dear Heavenly Father, thank You for hearing my prayer. Thank You for forgiving me of my sins and for loving me more than I can ever imagine. I know that You have loved me with an everlasting love since before the foundation of this world. I believe that You have good plans for me and good hopes for my future.

Show me all the places in the garden of my heart where my thoughts, attitudes, and actions need to be changed. Most of all, Lord, I desire that You will bring me into a deeper relationship with You. I pray that my time thinking about my future husband, my future wedding, and my future marriage will pale in comparison to preparing my heart and deepening my relationship with You—a relationship that will last for eternity.

I pray this in Your precious name, amen.

My Thoughts ON MY FUTURE HUSBAND AND ME HAVING HEARTS FOR GOD

DISCUSSION QUESTIONS

We wrote these questions for you to use as discussion starters in a small group or with your best friend. Also consider finding a notebook or journal and answering them for yourself, sharing your heart with God.

1. Describe the day your relationship with Jesus started.

2. If you haven't started a personal relationship with Jesus, what questions do you have that others in this group could help you with?

3. Many times, even though we love God, we find
    ourselves hiding from Him. Why do you hide? What
    does your hiding tell you that you need to change?

4. When did you first feel the truth that love begins
    in your heart? How has your idea of what love is
    changed?

5. Like Robin, do you ever see others with boyfriends and
    wish that was you? What helps during those times?

6. Tricia shared about her first boyfriend and first kiss.
    Many of us want the same thing—to feel as if we're
    Cinderella and the boy who likes us will be the one
    we'll be with forever. Do you think that's realistic?
    Why or why not?

7. Read Jeremiah 29:11–12. What stands out to you
    most about this scripture?

8. What's the difference between praying for God's plans to be done in your life and asking God to give you the desires of your heart?

9. How does it make you feel to know that, if you have entered into an eternal relationship with God, He sees you as His daughter?

10. In what ways do you think God is the perfect Father? How does seeing God as your loving Father give you more boldness as you pray?

11. What is the first thing you plan to pray for your future husband's heart?

12. When we pray for others, often we are changed. Why do you think this happens?

3

Pray

He Will Be a God Lover

> Love the LORD your God
> with all your heart
> and with all your soul
> and with all your strength.
>
> —DEUTERONOMY 6:5 (NIV)

Robin:

You've asked God to draw your future husband into His forever kingdom. Now pray that he will become a God Lover. No, I didn't say a *good* lover; I said a *God* Lover. We'll talk about the good lover part later. For now, let me explain what I mean by pointing out that the English language has only one word for love. Love, in all its forms, is a complex concept. Yet we have only one word for it. Doesn't seem quite adequate to cover all the bases, does it?

In comparison, the Hawaiian language has sixty-nine words for wind. This one element affects life on the islands in vastly different ways depending on what form it takes. You can imagine the difference between walking outside and feeling the light, "scattering flowers" wind (*Lupua*) as opposed to opening the front door and facing the (*Aiko'o*) "canoe eating" wind.

It sure would help if we had sixty-nine words for the various forms and meanings of love. There is a huge difference between a guy saying he loves you and saying he loves chili fries. At least there better be.

The first time a guy told me he loved me I was fifteen. His name was Davey, and he was sixteen. We met at a youth group event. He was really cute, and of course I loved the attention. We got along great, and it was a fun day. All too soon we had to say good-bye. Just before the church van I was riding in pulled out, Davey ran up alongside and frantically asked if anyone had a pen so he could write down my phone number. A pen was tossed to him, and as I called out the numbers, Davey wrote them on the palm of his hand.

I leaned out the open window. Our fingers touched, and as the van rolled away, he shouted, "I love you! I'll call you!" My girlfriends thought it was the most romantic gesture ever.

Davey called me every night for a couple of weeks. I don't remember what happened then, but the calls slowed before stopping altogether. Maybe he washed his hand and lost my number. Maybe he went to another youth group event and met another girl and told her he loved her. Maybe he just got busy and forgot all about me.

Did Davey mean it when he said he loved me? Maybe—in a fickle, short-lived, "scattering flowers" sort of way based on the high-flying emotions of the moment—he had a true twinge of love for me. But whatever he felt in the moment wasn't the sort of love that lasts.

Real, true, lasting love isn't rooted in emotions. True love comes from God's heart. His love transforms us deep down. As the Relentless Lover, God never stops pursuing us because we're His first love, and He wants us back.

God says: **"I will not forget you. See, I have written your name on my hand"** (Isaiah 49:15–16, NCV).

Instead of using ink from a borrowed pen as Davey did, God has written our names on the palm of His hand with borrowed nails and His own blood.

Now, that's real love, not the "scattering flowers" sort of fleeting love. God's ferocious affection for His children is a passionate, "canoe eating," life-changing, lay-down-His-life-for-you sort of love. God invites us...well, no, actually He commands us...to respond with the same level of passion and intensity in our love for Him. He created us to be God Lovers.

PRAY THAT YOUR FUTURE HUSBAND WILL LOVE GOD WITH A DEEP, UNSWERVING LOVE

When Jesus' disciples asked which was the most important commandment for them to follow, He replied: "Love the Lord your God with all your heart and with all your soul and with all your mind" (Matthew 22:37, NIV). Then He gave them the command to love others. God's model for deep and lasting love starts with our loving Him first, above all else.

This rich, unending love must be the soil in which our earthly love grows if we want it to last. Whenever a relationship is rooted in only human attraction and emotion, it doesn't have the ability to stretch those roots out deep enough to draw up the nutrients necessary to keep the love growing healthy and strong. Tricia discovered this early on in her relationship with Steven.

> I have loved you, my people,
> with an everlasting love.
> With unfailing love
> I have drawn you to myself.
>
> —JEREMIAH 31:3 (NLT)

Tricia:

All it took was that one kiss after the archery lesson, and I readily agreed to be Steven's girlfriend. We spent a lot of time together. We hiked in the hills behind our houses. We swung on the swings at the park. At night I would sneak out of my house to go to his. He would sneak out too, and we would sit on the grass in the warm summer night and watch the moon. And we always kissed.

When Steven wanted to go further than kissing, it only made sense. That's how things worked, right? I thought about the movies I had watched. The characters in them fell in love just like me, and then they slept together. Deep down I knew it wasn't right, but I didn't want to lose him. I didn't want him to find another girlfriend. I was sure if I gave Steven everything he wanted, we would stay together forever. Since I was so sure that I loved him and he loved me, I willingly gave myself to him.

But before the summer was over, Steven gave me some awful news. "My family is moving away."

My fairy-tale bubble burst. He was out of my life, and I was alone. I thought my heart would break.

My heart wasn't the only part of me that needed help. My emotions were a disaster. Not only had we been physically enmeshed, but we also had been emotionally enmeshed. My emotions were still tangled up with Steven, and I didn't know how to untangle them. I didn't know God was pursuing me and wanting to draw me into a close relationship rooted in His love. All I knew was that I hurt so deeply I wasn't sure I could ever love another guy again.

What About You?

Some of you know what this sort of heartache feels like because you've physically bonded with a guy. Others of you may not have given yourself to a guy physically, but you've bonded with him emotionally. Your future husband might be in that sort of relationship as well.

The inexplicable beauty of God's forever love is that, as the Relentless Lover, He never stops pursuing us because He always wants us back. He created us to be in close relationship with Him and will stop at nothing to restore that intimate relationship. Today, right now, is the time for you to make a radical change in your heart and life. Set your affection, your focus, and all your hopes on Christ. Trust Him. He bought you at a great price. He has dreams for you. Don't run from Him; run to Him. Knit your heart with His. Become a God Lover.

You are the God who buys me back.
Every time I run to the marketplace
And sell myself to a lie
You show up with a fistful of truth
And You buy me back.
Every time
Your word alone is enough
To remind me
And the slave driver
That with Your own flesh and blood
You have already paid for me
In full.
I belong to You, Great God.
You bought me back at a great price.
May I not run from You today.

—From Robin's journal

Oh, how you love the people,
> all his holy ones are palmed in your left hand.
> —Deuteronomy 33:3 (MSG)

HOW DO I PRAY THAT MY FUTURE HUSBAND WILL BE A GOD LOVER?

- Ask Jesus to help you break emotional and physical bonds with any guys to whom you've given yourself in the past. Jesus wants to be the One you love with your whole heart.
- Ask Jesus to help your future husband break off and be free of all emotional and physical bonds he has with old girlfriends.
- Pray that both of you will set your hearts and your affections fully on the Lord.
- Pray that both of you recognize that God is the Relentless Lover and that He wants your lives to be rooted in Him.

SHE PRAYED...GOD ANSWERED

I seriously began praying for the man I would marry when I was in college. There was a period of time when I was prompted to pray that God would show my future husband that the relationship he was in was harmful and destructive. I wrote out a series of prayers in my journal asking

God to give this man—whom I didn't know yet—strength
and resolve to end the relationship. I felt so strongly that
this is what I should be praying that I prayed these
prayers every night—and I wrote about them in my journal.

Years later, when I began dating my husband, the topic
of past relationships came up. He only had one—during
those same months I had prayed so intently for him. It was
destructive, and he ended the relationship right around the
time my burden to pray those prayers stopped. The dates
listed in my old journals beside my written prayers perfectly coincided with the months he was in that
relationship.

I will never forget the look of amazement on
Michael's face when I told him about my old journals
and those prayers. He was stunned and overcome with
emotion at the same time. The fact that God could
prompt me to pray about specific circumstances in his life
when I didn't even know him was amazing. Both of
us could see how God was shedding His grace and love on
us and knitting us together even before we met.
—Shannon P.

We know what real love is because
Jesus gave up his life for us.

—1 JOHN 3:16 (NLT)

A Prayer for My Future Husband

Dear Lord Jesus, it's so amazing that You can see my future husband now. You know him. You love him.

Lord, since You know the man You have designed for me, I pray that any other relationship will be unappealing to him. I pray that if he is giving away a part of his heart, his emotions, or his body, You will show him Your better way.

Most of all I pray he'll be a God Lover. Not only do I ask that You distract and keep him from other, harmful relationships but also that You draw him closer to You. May his heart be so full of You that he doesn't need anything, anyone else…until the time You appoint to bring me into his life.

And for every day of his life, hold him in the palm of Your hand. Amen.

A Prayer for Me

Dear Lord Jesus, forgive me for all the times I've looked for love from others when I should have looked for that love from You. Forgive me for giving bits of myself to others—mind, soul, spirit, and body—when I should have saved all of me for You. I know, Lord, Your plan for our lives includes saving what is most precious for the one we dedicate ourselves to, but I have failed in so many ways. I thank You, Lord Jesus, that You have come to forgive me and to make me pure as snow. I thank You that, when You forgive me, those sins are forgotten forever. It is like they never happened.

Thank You that only You can untangle my heart from the unhealthy relationships I've involved myself in. Begin untangling now, Lord, and don't stop until You're done. I want to fall in love with You with all my heart, soul, strength, and mind. I want to be known as a woman who is a God Lover. Amen.

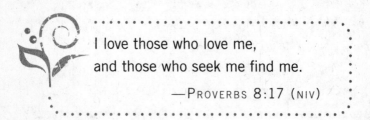

I love those who love me,
and those who seek me find me.

—PROVERBS 8:17 (NIV)

My Thoughts ON MY FUTURE HUSBAND
AND ME BEING GOD LOVERS

DISCUSSION QUESTIONS

1. How does it make you feel to think that your future husband may be in a relationship with someone else

right now? In what ways does this urge you on to pray
for your future husband?

2. If you are—or have been—in a relationship with
    someone, what do you think your future husband will
    think about that? How does thinking ahead to the day
    you'll meet your future husband make you reconsider
    your actions now?

3. Have you ever had a guy write your number on his
    hand or do something equally romantic? How did it
    make you feel?

4. How does it make you feel to know that God has
    written your name on the palm of His hand, and it
    will never wash off or fade away?

5. Tricia confessed that she became sexually intimate
    with her first boyfriend because she thought that's
    what people did; movies, books, and examples in her
    life showed her this. She also didn't want to lose her
    boyfriend. What other reasons cause young women
    to choose to be sexually active?

6. Physical bonding wasn't the only attachment discussed in this chapter. In what ways do we become emotionally attached to another person?

7. How can God help us to break emotional bonds?

8. Read Jeremiah 31:3. How do you feel when you think about God drawing you to Himself? In what ways have you known this to be true in your own life?

9. Shannon shared about praying that her future husband would end a destructive relationship and later found out her prayers had helped him during that time. Have you ever felt drawn to pray for your future husband in a specific way? Did you pray?

10. In Robin's journal, she wrote about selling herself to lies. What lies have you sold yourself to? How does God's truth stand up to those lies?

4

Pray

for

Patience

I wait for the LORD, my whole being waits,
and in his word I put my hope.

—PSALM 130:5 (NIV)

Robin:

Yes, I know. Don't ever pray for patience because God will give you trials to produce that patience in you. You've heard the same advice, haven't you?

Here's a great reason to pray for patience. It's the first quality of true love listed in 1 Corinthians 13.

LOVE IS PATIENT

Step one, lesson one, in the adventure of experiencing true love is patience. It's an essential quality needed before you marry and absolutely required if you're going to stay married.

Any couple who remained chaste until their wedding night will tell you how agonizingly difficult it was to be in love and yet committed to being patient and waiting. I don't just mean waiting to give yourself physically to the one you love. I'm also thinking about the difficulty of waiting for the right one to show up. Love requires a lot of patience before, during, and after the walk down the white runner to the altar.

If it's true love, as in God's forever kind of love, that you want to experience, then patience is going to be one of the key ingredients in this recipe for bliss.

> Wait for the LORD;
>   be strong and take heart
>   and wait for the LORD.
> —Psalm 27:14 (NIV)

As a teen I balanced the angst of waiting by expressing myself on paper. That's how I came up with the idea of Christy's writing a letter to her future husband in *Island Dreamer*. On my sixteenth birthday I also wrote my first letter to my future husband. I told him that I was praying for him and that I was waiting for him. I folded up the letter and tucked it into a shoebox. I hid the box under my bed and started to wait...wait for my first real date, my first real boyfriend, my first real kiss.

Christy Miller's Diary Entry
to Her Future Husband

I turned sixteen today, and I know it may seem weird writing this to you now, but this letter is sort of my way of making a promise to you in writing.

Maybe I already know you, or maybe we haven't met yet. Either way, I want to save myself for you. I want my whole self, my heart and body and everything, to be a present I'll give you on our wedding day.

I don't care how long it takes or how hard it gets, but I promise you I won't let anybody else "unwrap" me, so on our wedding night I'll be the kind of gift you'll be happy to receive.

I know I have a lot of years ahead of me before we get married, whoever you are. That's why I want to make this promise now, so that no matter whom I go out with, I'll always think of myself as a present I want to give to you alone one day.

I also want to start to pray for you, wherever you are, whoever you are, that God will be preparing you for me and that you'll save all of yourself for me too.

I already love you.

Your future wife,

Christina Juliet Miller

—From the Christy Miller Series, vol. 2, *Island Dreamer*

Pray for Your Future Husband to Develop Patience as He Waits for You

Then I got sick. Really sick. I had to leave school and stay in bed for almost three months. A tutor came to the house a few hours each week so I could keep up with my studies and finish my sophomore year of high school.

By the time summer came and I was starting to feel better, my closest girlfriends had steady boyfriends. Even though I was well enough to go do things again, I wasn't included in their weekend plans since I didn't have a boyfriend. I stayed home and waited for my social life to begin.

Waiting is awful.

However, the consequences for not waiting can be worse. Tricia has a few things to say about that.

> Spread out your petition before God, and then say, "Thy will, not mine, be done." The sweetest lesson I have learned in God's school is to let the Lord choose for me.
>
> —Dwight L. Moody

Tricia:

My sophomore year of high school I was a cheerleader. One day after school, when I was hanging out with the five other cheerleaders, I noticed a new guy on the football team. We were supposed to be practicing…but we found the guys leaving the field in their practice uniforms far more interesting.

"I think his name is Robbie," my friend Jennifer told me. "He just moved here."

Robbie glanced over as he walked away, and his eyes met mine. He had blond hair and a great smile. He reminded me of Steven in a way, and my heart ached with loneliness. I had experienced love, but I had lost it. I wanted that feeling of being loved and accepted again.

I turned back to my friends, and my body went through the motions of the cheer, but my mind was on Robbie. He was cuter than most of the guys at our high school, and I wanted him to be my boyfriend. I wanted to be seen at his side. I wanted to feel desired again.

After Steven moved away, I started to date someone else right away. After him came another boyfriend, but he didn't last very long either. Whenever I had a boyfriend, it seemed I was always on the lookout for who would take his place if things didn't work out.

When I found someone new, like Robbie, I spent most of my time with him or talking to him on the telephone. I didn't feel whole if I wasn't with that person. I felt lonely whenever we were separated. I was also worried whenever we were apart. What if he found someone else? I wanted to keep my boyfriend's attention, keep his love.

When school started, I found out Robbie was in my drafting class, which was perfect. We sat next to each other and talked as we sketched out house plans for our class project. Robbie and I talked a lot and dated soon after that. Being with him stirred the same emotions I had felt when I was with Steven, and within a few months I gave myself completely to Robbie.

But giving myself away led me to decisions I never thought I'd have to make. At age fifteen, less than two years after I had my first kiss, I found myself pregnant.

Me? How could this be possible?

From that moment my life would never be the same.

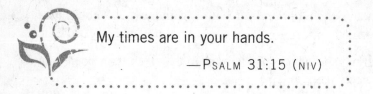

My times are in your hands.

—Psalm 31:15 (NIV)

What About You?

How are you doing with waiting on the Lord for His timing in your life? Are you finding it more and more difficult to be patient as the months and years roll by? It's hard to be patient when you watch your girlfriends dating and getting married yet no one is pursuing you.

What is it that the Lord is asking you to work on in your life during this season? Please don't compromise your standards. Don't start making excuses to justify why you're settling for actions or relationships that you know in your heart aren't what you want your life to be about. How can you change that destructive behavior today? What are the new choices you need to start making?

Most importantly, be at peace. See this time as an opportunity for God to develop His patience in you. And don't forget: love is patient.

Will you get married one day? Statistics say you will. We all know that staying married is a whole lot more important than just getting married. How you spend this stretch of waiting and allowing God to develop His patience in you will only benefit you during the difficult times that all married couples go through.

Here's a visual image that might help you during this season of patience building. Think of your life as being like a ball of yarn. Imagine pulling out the first few inches of yarn and viewing that small stretch as the amount of time you are spending now as you wait to be married. Now look at the rest of the ball of yarn. That's a lot of inches. You have the rest of your life to spend with the right man whom God brings into your life. These first few inches of yarn are nothing compared to the rest of the rolled-up ball waiting to be unraveled. You can wait that long. Really. You can.

> We also have joy with our troubles, because we know that these troubles produce patience. And patience produces character, and character produces hope. And this hope will never disappoint us, because God has poured out his love to fill our hearts.
> —Romans 5:3–5 (NCV)

How would you say you're doing during these few inches of waiting time? Are you watching and praying, as Jesus asked His disciples to do (see Matthew 26:41)? Are you trusting God and waiting? Or are you running ahead?

Perhaps you've prayed and prayed, but God hasn't answered. Your prayers seem like bulbs planted in a winter garden. Each time you check for results, all you see is barrenness, debris, and frost. You doubt the warmth of the faith you felt when you first planted the prayers in a season of light and hope.

Patience, dear God Lover. Nothing is wrong with your prayers. Leave all of them safely hidden with the Lord. Hold fast to the hope that He has heard and is at work in the garden of your heart. One bright spring morning you will be stunned when you see what God's resurrection power has done with those requests you buried so long ago.

One day Jesus told his disciples a story to show that they should always pray and never give up.

—LUKE 18:1 (NLT)

How Do I Pray for God to Develop Patience in My Future Husband?

- Pray he will turn to God and that God's peace will help him be inwardly calm and willing to wait.

- Pray he will have a quiet and steady faithfulness to God.
- Pray he will be content in every state in which he finds himself.
- Pray his eyes will be focused on things to come rather than things he wished he had now.
- Pray he will not push for answers before the time is right.
- Pray he will trust God's sense of timing.
- Pray he will be reminded of all the times God has been patient with him.
- Pray he waits with hope and expectancy.

Of course, as you pray these things for your future husband, be sure to pray the same for yourself. Patience is like holding a closed bud of promise in your hand. Imagine that closed, white rose in your mind. Consider allowing each petal to unfold slowly, in its own way. Can you see the beauty of each stage? Can you see God's hand wrapped around yours, watching the unfolding with you?

Rejoice in your hope,
be patient in tribulation,
be constant in prayer.

—ROMANS 12:12 (RSV)

SHE PRAYED...GOD ANSWERED

For me, waiting was a constant series of looking at every guy who showed interest (and some who didn't), just in case. I didn't want to miss what God might be showing me. I had made a very detailed list of what I wanted, and I mean *detailed*. I prayed over it, ending my prayer with, "This is what I want; now please give me what I need."

I had started to pray for my husband years ago, and after realizing that none of the men I was meeting lived up to my standards, I gave up.

That's when God showed His sense of humor, and I met Jackson. He was not what I thought I'd asked for, except he was, because I went through my list and checked everything off. Down to the blue eyes. Now, sixteen years later, we are still goofy in love.
—Tracey

Where Are You?
I have waited so patiently.
Where are you?
They said if I would wait as if I was not expecting
        anything to happen, you would arrive.
Where are you?
I have been dreaming of you for years yet still my
        dreams don't become reality.
Where are you?
I have been writing you letters and saving them for you.

Where are you?

Everyone around me is getting this question answered
      while I sit alone.

Where are you?

Are you asking the same question of me?

I'm right here.

Where are you?

My hand is lonely without yours to fill it.

How long must I wait?

I'm ready. Are you?

Waiting… My life feels like an endless line of waiting.

Where is my fast pass?

How can I pass go and collect you?

Why does it feel like I always get the shoots when
      everyone else is getting the ladders?

Where are you?

—Rachel Gunn

A Prayer for My Future Husband

Dear Lord, I pray that, as the years pass, the best game my future husband will win is the waiting game. I pray that he will have long vision to look ahead, waiting for me with expectation instead of looking at his current moment with a sense of missing out. I pray that he will be so filled with Your love that it will weigh him down. Anchor him in Your Word and make the thought of running around and searching for temporary answers unappealing.

Father, Your Word says that patience comes with trials, and I pray that, as my future husband walks through the trials of life, he will sense You walking with him and at times carrying him. And may the patience he develops not only help him wait for me...may it also prepare him for life with me. Amen.

A Prayer for Me

Dear Lord, I pray that instead of looking around at each new guy who enters my life and always wondering, projecting on him what I think the future might hold, I will lift my eyes to You. Instead of feeling envy when I see all the fun my friends seem to be having in their relationships, teach me to share their joy as a true friend. Open my eyes to the pain they face when things don't turn out as they had hoped. And with Your love in me, help me to comfort them, even in their pain.

I am impatient, Lord. I want what I want when I want it. Show me the beauty and peace that patience can produce in my life. Teach me how to wait on You. Help me to trust that You have the answers and will reveal those answers in Your good and proper time.

Forgive me, Lord, for all the times I haven't waited but have stepped outside of Your will. Forgive me for taking matters into my own hands and letting my sometimes foolish heart lead me in the wrong direction and away from You and Your heart's desires for my life. In all the ways my impatience has turned to sin, forgive me. Make me clean. Strengthen me as I wait.

I ask this in the mighty name of Jesus, amen.

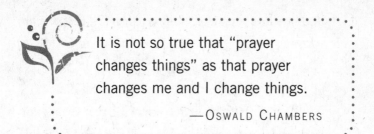

It is not so true that "prayer changes things" as that prayer changes me and I change things.

—OSWALD CHAMBERS

My Thoughts ON MY FUTURE HUSBAND AND ME BEING PATIENT

DISCUSSION QUESTIONS

1. Why is being patient so hard for us in today's society?

2. In what ways do you run ahead, trying to find your future husband, instead of waiting for God's timing?

3. God says love is patient. How is patience an expression of love?

4. Read Psalm 31:15. How does knowing that God holds your times in His hands help you? What do you think He would say to you about those times, if you were sitting face to face right now?

5. Robin started to write letters to her future husband on her sixteenth birthday. Have you written a letter to your future husband? What is appealing about that idea? Why might you hesitate over the idea?

6. Once Steven moved away, Tricia looked for guys to take his place and to fill the void inside. Do you know any young women desperate to be loved? Where does their desperation come from?

7. Once Tricia gave herself physically to a guy, it became easier for her to continue down that path. How do you think patience would have helped in that situation?

8. Do you ever ask the same questions Rachel did in her poem, "Where Are You?" What line stood out to you the most?

9. What do you think are some of the hardest things for your future husband to be patient about? How can you pray for those struggles?

10. How could lifting your vision to God and focusing on Him help you be patient in all areas of life?

11. What things can your friends pray for you concerning patience?

5

Pray for Understanding

By wisdom a house is built,
and through understanding
it is established.

—Proverbs 24:3 (NIV)

Robin:

A little understanding goes a long way in any relationship.

Have you ever noticed how easy it is to be critical of someone or judgmental of a decision that person made? But then you receive one more piece of information—an additional glimpse of the bigger picture—and suddenly you're not so critical. That's the gift of understanding.

But it is the spirit in a person,
the breath of the Almighty,
that gives them understanding.

—Job 32:8 (NIV)

By the end of my freshman year of college, I was pretty sure I had met The One. His name was Mike, and sometime in the middle of my sophomore year, I wrote another letter to my future husband to add to the five or six letters I had written to him over the years. This time, though, I boldly filled in his name. "Mike, I know you're the one. I love you. I know you're getting close to proposing, and I can't wait to one day give you these letters so you can see how I've been praying for you for all these years."

Mike graduated from the Christian college we both attended, and a few months later, he proposed. The week before I started my junior year of college we announced our engagement at a party with all our friends. I was the happiest woman on the planet.

That night Mike and I went back to my parents' house, and I decided I couldn't wait until after we were married to give the letters to him. I went to my old room, pulled out the shoebox where I had lovingly kept the letters, and presented them to him.

He slowly read the first one, then the second and the third. His reaction surprised me. He didn't get choked up or indicate that he cherished my every word as I thought he would.

"What are you thinking?" I asked cautiously.

"I'm surprised," he said. "Writing these letters is a romantic gesture."

We had been together for more than a year. I knew by his expression he was thinking more than he was saying. I asked him what else he thought.

"It's just that you have a tendency to overspiritualize things," he said. "Don't you think that writing letters to a person years before you've even met him is along the lines of fairy-tale thinking? I don't understand why you would do something like this."

I realize now that Mike didn't understand who I was—the person God created me to be. I've spent most of my life thinking up stories that have happy endings and writing them in such a way that the spiritual side of life comes through and gives readers hope. Mike didn't understand the ways God had gifted me or what God had called me to do. And I had very little understanding of Mike's past, his struggles, or his goals for the future.

At the time all I knew was that I loved Mike and he loved me. That was all we needed to understand, right?

Pray That Your Future Husband Has Understanding

Mike kept all the letters. And I kept trying to change. I thought I needed to become more like the person he thought I should be. I worked hard to conform to the standard he thought we should establish for our lives together. Our engagement was a lot of work.

Then, six months into our engagement, Mike said he couldn't marry me. My wedding dress was hanging in the closet, the invitations were ready to go to the printer's, and the church had been reserved and paid for.

His precise words on a cold afternoon in February pierced my heart. "I don't love you, Robin. I thought I did, but I don't.

It would be a terrible mistake for me to commit myself to you for life."

"Mike, what are saying?"

"I can't marry you." Tears welled in his eyes. "One day you'll thank me for making this decision for both of us."

I was devastated. I couldn't believe he had come to this conclusion. Not after all we had been through together over the past two years. We had worked so hard at trying to build a strong relationship.

Everything I believed about happy endings was demolished. Why would God allow such pain and rejection in my life? Hadn't I promised to follow God, serve Him, and love Him with all my heart? Hadn't I made all the right decisions for purity and integrity? What had I accomplished when I spent those hours praying for my future husband and writing out my prayers for him late at night when this was the result?

How could I ever trust my judgment again?

I sold my car, emptied my savings account, packed my bags, and ran away to Europe for four months. I thought that would help dull the pain that greeted me every morning when I awoke. But all the ache of the loss and rejection climbed into my backpack and stayed with me every step of the way. I don't know how my traveling companions put up with me.

In years to come, I would see how this painful experience produced in me a deeper understanding of others. My editor once asked how I was able to accurately describe the feelings going on inside the characters in my novels. All I could say was,

"I became familiar with love, loss, and longing early on in life. I understand how it feels."

> GOD, come close. Come quickly!
> Open your ears—it's my voice you're hearing!
> Treat my prayer as sweet incense rising;
> my raised hands are my evening prayers.
> —Psalm 141:1–2 (MSG)

Tricia:

The doctor's words shocked me. "Tricia, you're pregnant."

I remember later that day lying in bed and not believing it could be true. The first thing I felt was fear. My parents knew, Robbie knew, but I didn't want anyone else to know that I'd been sexually active.

Robbie wanted me to have an abortion. He wasn't ready to be a dad, and he made it clear that it would end our relationship if I chose to keep the baby. My parents were supportive—they said they would help either way—but they left the decision up to me.

I went to counseling, even though I was fairly sure I knew what I wanted to do.

"You're pretty young." The counselor looked up from my file. "Your boyfriend is young too."

"Yes, I know."

"Do you feel you're ready to care for a child? This is a huge commitment."

I shook my head. No, I didn't feel ready at all.

"I think an abortion would be the right choice," she said.

I listened. I wasn't sure. I knew that if I stayed pregnant, I'd have a baby. But I sensed that I shouldn't have an abortion.

The woman must have noticed my hesitancy. "You know, at this stage of pregnancy, there are just a few cells. The procedure would just scrape those away so they won't grow. It'll be done quickly, then you can go home, and this whole thing will be over."

That sounded like a good idea. I looked at the woman and tried to grasp the hope she offered.

Yet when the procedure happened, I didn't experience relief. Instead, I felt shame. As the weeks and months passed, I felt numb. I'd been looking for love, but I had found only pain— the pain of aborting a child I would never know. And the pain in my relationships with guys. Each time I gave myself away to another guy, there was less of me to hold on to. The bonds I was trying to create ripped away a part of my heart.

A deep sadness weighed on my chest by my sixteenth birthday. "Sweet sixteen and never been kissed" couldn't have been less true for me. I didn't even feel sweet. Darkness hung over me. I had given everything and had received nothing but heartache in return. I was still dating Robbie at the time, but we were having trouble. He no longer made me happy. Nothing made me happy.

Months after I had chosen the abortion, I was having dinner at my grandma's house, and her pastor and his wife were there. The pastor's wife was wearing a pin on her shirt that showed baby footprints.

"That's really cute," I said.

"It's the same size as the feet of a ten-week-old fetus," Darlyne told me. "So tiny, yet so perfect."

I felt as if someone had punched me in the gut. I struggled to suck in a breath, but I couldn't catch one, and I quickly walked away. The woman at the clinic had told me it was just a few cells. She had lied. My worries over what people would think and my fears of keeping my boyfriend had caused me to make a haunting decision. I couldn't get that image of those little feet out of my mind. My baby had had a body and a beating heart.

I was angry that I had been lied to. I had been deceived in so many ways.

Sometimes at night I would think about my future husband, but the fanciful dreams that I had years before were gone. Those happy thoughts had been replaced by worry.

Would I ever find someone to love me?

What would he think if he knew about my abortion?

I had given so much of myself away. Was there any more of me left to give?

I wished I had waited. I wished I had been more patient in my search for love. I wished I understood what I was choosing when I decided on an abortion. I wished I had understood what I was truly doing when I gave someone all of me.

Have I forever ruined my chances to find true love? No one will want me now. No one will understand.

WHAT ABOUT YOU?

Sometimes you think you know what you're doing—what you're choosing—but later the truth is known, is felt. Then, when things don't turn out as you had hoped, you wonder if God is even out there, or if He cares.

In all your relationships—the good, the bad, the confusing—are you seeing that there is often more to the situation than how things first appeared? God knows everything about us. He understands every thought and feeling before we even think it or feel it. Nothing is wasted in His economy, even though we don't see how that's possible at the time.

Take heart. God sees the big picture. Rest in Him, and give Him time to reveal His plans for you.

Above all, trust in the slow work of God.
We are quite naturally impatient in everything to reach
    the end without delay.
We should like to skip the intermediate stages.
We are impatient of being on the way to something
    unknown, something new...
Only God could say what this new spirit gradually
    forming within you will be.
Give our Lord the benefit of believing that His hand is
    leading you,
and accept the anxiety of feeling yourself in suspense
    and incomplete.
    —Pierre Teilhard de Chardin

My prayer is that light will flood your hearts and that you will understand the hope that was given to you when God chose you. Then you will discover the glorious blessings that will be yours together with all of God's people.

    —Ephesians 1:18 (CEV)

HOW DO I PRAY THAT MY FUTURE HUSBAND WOULD HAVE UNDERSTANDING?

- Pray that God's light will flood his heart.
- Pray that your future husband will seek God and try to understand what God is doing in his life.
- Pray that he will have a tender heart that will be understanding of your past mistakes.
- Pray that you will be understanding of his.
- Pray that, if he has his heart broken, he will be surrounded by good friends who will support him during the healing process.
- Pray that in each of his relationships he will develop an understanding heart and always believe that God has a different and better plan.

SHE PRAYED...GOD ANSWERED

When I was in high school, I prayed for and wrote to my future husband. Stopping to put my feelings down on paper was helpful during times when I wanted to express love with reckless abandon. I wanted desperately to give my heart but knew I shouldn't, because it wasn't time. My parents had given me a purity ring. On my wedding day my father walked me down the aisle. Before placing my hand in the hand of my groom, my father asked in front of all our guests if I had kept my promise to save myself for my husband. He knew the answer was yes. When I declared publicly that I had, he took the promise ring from my finger so that it would be ready to receive the wedding ring from my husband.

Now, after three kids and ten years of marriage, the funny thing is that my husband still hasn't read the letters. Not because he doesn't care, but the timing just hasn't been right. And that's fine with me. I see now that the exercise of writing the letters was more for me than for my husband to read them. Those expressive letters helped keep me focused and pure-hearted until it was time to fully give myself to my worthy and honorable husband with reckless abandon.
—Natalie

When you pray, rather let your heart be without words than your words without heart.

—JOHN BUNYAN

A PRAYER FOR MY FUTURE HUSBAND

Dear Lord, I know there may be times in my future husband's life when he doesn't understand what's going on. There may be relationships that bring him hurt. There may be situations in which he doesn't know what to do or where to turn. I pray that in those times, he will turn to You, and You will give him direction and peace.

As he has questions and is making decisions, I pray he will turn to You for understanding. I know that the more understanding he has now in situations big or small, the better he will be prepared for marriage.

Finally, I pray You will give him a heart of compassion. I pray that he will be understanding about the mistakes I've made.

In the name of Your Son, amen.

A PRAYER FOR ME

Dear Lord, just as I've made mistakes, I know it's likely that my future husband has too. I pray that even now you will prepare my heart to deal with the ways he has fallen short.

Lots of things are happening in my life that I don't understand. Why does my heart have longings for a relationship that won't be fulfilled for years? Why do people have to hurt or disappoint me? Why do I hurt and disappoint myself?

I pray that You will give me understanding to handle life—now and in the future. The one thing I do understand, dear Lord,

is Your love. I understand You love me more than anyone else does.
I understand You have good plans for the future. Thank You.
 I love You. Amen.

For this reason, since the day we heard about you, we
have not stopped praying for you. We continually ask
God to fill you with the knowledge of his will through
all the wisdom and understanding that the Spirit gives.
—Colossians 1:9 (NIV)

My Thoughts ON MY FUTURE HUSBAND AND ME DEVELOPING UNDERSTANDING

DISCUSSION QUESTIONS

1. Think of a time when you didn't understand something at first, but later it became clear (like multiplica-

tion problems or how to drive a car). How did you feel
when you finally understood?

2. When Robin was in her relationship with Mike, she
wanted to change to gain his approval. How did her
understanding of the situation change over time?

3. How did Mike's response to Robin's letters reveal
what he thought about her? In what ways do others'
responses help us to understand more about them
and our relationship with them?

4. Concerning your future husband, what do you wish
you understood? How can you use that longing for
understanding in your prayers?

5. What do you hope your future husband understands
about you?

6. Read Ephesians 1:8. How does hope help with
understanding?

7. Do you think that when we are in desperate situations, such as Tricia was with her pregnancy, that we are more likely to cling to whatever people tell us is the solution? Why or why not?

8. What decisions led to Tricia's pain?

9. How does knowing that God sees the big picture help you? What can you do to develop the habit of turning to Him for understanding?

10. Just as you have made mistakes, no doubt your future husband has too. What are specific things you can pray for that will help you to deal with his mistakes?

6

Pray for Trust

> But I trusted in, relied on,
> and was confident in You, O Lord;
> I said, You are my God.
>
> —Psalm 31:14 (amp)

Robin:

Perhaps you've noticed the three-way relationship that comes into focus when you start to pray for your future husband. As you pray that he will be a God Lover, you quickly see that your own relationship with the Lord has room to grow too. You ask God to develop patience in your future mate and soon realize that God is using the challenges in your life to develop patience in you. You pray for your future husband to have understanding, and your sense of compassion grows.

Do you see the triangular relationship that is formed through prayer? You, your future husband, and God. God is at the top of the triangle, while you and your future husband are at the corner points at the bottom. The closer each of you becomes to God, the shorter the distance between the two of you. By praying for the man you will marry one day, you are drawing closer to the Lord. You, God, and your future husband—the three of you already are being braided together at the heart level through the invisible realm of prayer. Cool, isn't it? The three of you are entwined in an eternal relationship; yet you might not even have met your future husband.

> A cord of three strands is not quickly torn apart.
> —Ecclesiastes 4:12 (NASB)

BELIEF IS THE BASIS OF TRUST

I learned a lot about trust during the four months I traveled in Europe after Mike broke our engagement. One of those months I attended an Upward Bound program at a Capernwray Bible School in Austria. The highlight of the program was the final week, when we hiked through the Alps like the von Trapp family and learned how to rock climb. I went through the training and watched half of the other seventeen students successfully cinch the carabiner, grip the rope, and back over the side of the unyielding rock as our trainer, Gernot, belayed them to the open area below.

When my turn came to rappel off the face of the sheer cliff, I was fitted with the proper gear and given final instructions. But I couldn't do it.

"Trust me," Gernot said.

All I needed to do was take the first step. From all sides I was being coached on what I needed to do, but I still couldn't do it. I couldn't convince my body to believe that I could defy gravity, lean back, and depend on only a rope to keep me from falling to my death. I was paralyzed with fear.

Gernot pulled me aside. He unfastened the rope and released me from the harness. "Tomorrow," he said with quiet patience and understanding.

That night our group stayed in a nearby chalet. Everyone who had belayed down the cliff arrived first. I had to hike a long and more treacherous route to reach the chalet. Gernot walked every step with me. When we arrived, the rest of the group was rested and ready for dinner.

My feet ached from the long hike as I tucked them under the wooden table. The others spoke energetically about their rock-climbing experiences. They discussed how they didn't believe they could do such a thing until they tried the ropes and tested their own strength. One of the girls described how she felt when she took that first step. It had clearly been a life-changing experience for her.

I had missed out on the experience. I'd also missed out on the more direct route to the chalet because I had chosen not to believe. I had withheld my trust, and that choice hurt not only me but also Gernot, who walked with me all the way like a patient shepherd. He couldn't move forward until I moved forward.

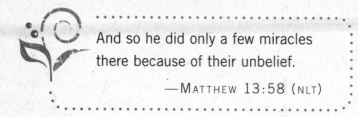

And so he did only a few miracles there because of their unbelief.

—Matthew 13:58 (nlt)

Since the painful breakup with Mike, I had found it easy to choose not to trust anyone—even God. That secret lack of trust and belief was affecting every area of my life. I pulled back in all my relationships. I found reasons to complain or to be critical of others instead of being understanding and patient. Without realizing it, I had positioned myself as a wounded victim so that others would feel sorry for me.

That evening, as the snowflakes pressed themselves against the thick-paned windows and peered into the chalet at our bowls of steaming soup and crusty brown bread, I decided the fear needed to go away. Jesus came that I might have life and have it more abundantly. To experience that abundance, I knew I needed to believe He was in control of all things. He was trustworthy.

The next day I put my renewed sense of trust to the test. I stepped into the harness, held on to the rope, and told Gernot I believed he would support me. Then I leaned back into nothing but crisp Alpine air and felt something deep inside coming back to life. It was my heart! In choosing to trust, I was opening myself up to all the possibilities God might have designed for me, including falling in love again.

What I didn't know was that I had met my future husband two years earlier. I was just too focused on Mike, and the person

I thought Mike wanted me to be, to pay any attention to Ross. Now that I was learning to trust again, my eyes were opening right along with the opening of my heart.

Oh, what a wide, wonderful world brimming with vast possibilities lies open before us once we stop letting fear make all the decisions for us! Once the fear, like a strangling vine, had been extracted from the garden of my heart, I discovered wide open, sunny places where belief and trust had room to grow.

Tricia also went through a dark time when she didn't dare to trust anyone or believe her future would again hold joy or peace. Through those painful times for both of us, the Lord was very close. We couldn't see Him. We didn't recognize the ways He was caring for us or calling to us. But He never left. He never gave up on us because of our unbelief. For both of us, God sent caring believers to shepherd us during the difficult season; through their love and kindness, He demonstrated His trustworthiness toward us.

> Trust in the LORD with all your heart
>> and lean not on your own understanding;
> in all your ways submit to him,
>> and he will make your paths straight.
> —Proverbs 3:5–6 (NIV)

Tricia:

Something inside me died the day I chose to abort my baby. After that I felt like a zombie, walking around without joy or peace. I didn't want to cry—after all, I was the one who chose to have an abortion. I didn't want to regret or feel the shame, but when I blocked those emotions, I blocked *all* emotions.

Robbie and I continued our relationship, but in a way I hated him for getting me pregnant and for insisting I abort. He broke up with me and dated other girls. Then we got back together. I broke up with him and dated other guys, but in the end I went back to him. I chose an abortion so I could keep Robbie; if I let our relationship fail, I reasoned that I had sacrificed my child's life for nothing.

Robbie and I continued our physical relationship. Every time we were together, I hoped to feel the same excitement I had experienced with Steven that first time. Yet my mind, heart, and body all seemed numb.

A year after my abortion, I found myself pregnant again. I wasn't too surprised. I wasn't trying to get pregnant, but I wasn't trying too hard not to either. Right away Robbie said I should have another abortion. I refused. More than anything I wanted this child—someone to love and someone who would love me.

When word got out that I was pregnant, I quit cheerleading, and after a few weeks, I quit my job and dropped out of school. The morning sickness made me feel horrible, but even worse I couldn't handle the stares and whispers at school or work. Everyone now knew the type of girl I was, and I hated that.

After a few weeks Robbie and I broke up again, and he started to date someone else. I wanted to crawl into a dark cave and never come out. That's basically what I did.

As my pregnancy progressed, I pretty much dropped out of

life. Two days a week I went to a community high school to finish the rest of my credits for graduation, but most of the time I stayed in bed. I slept in, watched television, and then stayed up late watching more television. My friends were going on with their senior year, and I had never felt so alone.

During that time the ladies from my mother and grandmother's Bible study group invited me to join them. I refused. The last thing I wanted was to study the Bible. I knew what it would say about my sin, and I didn't want to hear it. How could God love me after what I had done? My mom kept inviting me, but I kept refusing. Once the pastor's wife, Darlyne, came by to invite me too.

"We would love to have you," Darlyne said. I was still in bed in my pajamas, and she stood in my room's doorway.

"No thanks," I said in a growl that made it clear she shouldn't ask again.

"Well, at least may I pray for you?"

"Fine, whatever." I rolled over and turned my back to her. I heard Darlyne's soft footsteps on the carpet, as she approached my bed. She didn't touch me, but I could hear her whispered prayers. I tried to sleep, to pretend she wasn't there. It didn't work. I tried to pretend I was mad, but deep down I kind of appreciated that she cared. After a while I heard her walk away. There was no lecture or sermon. I didn't know what to think of that.

My mom didn't ease up. She continued to invite me to the Bible study every week. "Come on, give it a try," my mom urged me one day.

I shrugged. "Okay. I guess, but I might just take a nap."

That's what I did. I fell asleep in the La-Z-Boy recliner, as the women talked about the Bible.

The next week, though, I stayed awake and listened. I also spent time talking to the other women.

"Tricia, we would like to give you a baby shower," Gayle told me. "What do you need?"

I listed a few things, and the women took notes. They also asked me to put together a guest list. They talked about my growing belly and told me their labor stories. I had thought they would condemn me, but instead I felt loved and cared for.

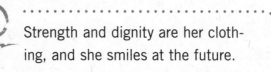

Strength and dignity are her clothing, and she smiles at the future.

—Proverbs 31:25 (NASB)

The next day when I woke up at 11 a.m., I thought about those women. They had every right to talk about me, to condemn me, to point fingers at me, but they didn't. I also thought about the church I used to go to. Another woman used to love me like these women seemed to—my Sunday school teacher when I was small. The pastor always cared for me and gave me a hug. I smiled when I remembered the twinkle in his eyes.

If the women at the Bible study can love me, I thought, *what about God? Does He still love me after all I've done? Can I trust Him?*

A Sunday school song came to mind. *Jesus loves me! This I know, for the Bible tells me so.* The song played through my mind. Looking for love, I had come to a place of feeling completely unloved. I was ready to do things differently. My way hadn't worked.

I rolled onto my side and wrapped my arms around my large stomach. *Dear God, I've screwed up big time. If You can do anything with my life, please do.*

It was a simple prayer, but hope flooded my heart and filled my chest. Some of the heaviness I had been carrying around for so long was gone. A smile filled my face and with it came tears—not ones of sadness, but ones of joy. God *did* love me. I could feel it deep inside. That was my first step of trust.

After that, I started to read my Bible and go to church. I still had layer after layer of pain inside, but each day that I spent time with God, I felt Him peel away those hurts.

One day, as I sat on my bed and leaned against the wall, I thought about my future. *Where am I going? How am I going to get there?* I pulled out one of my school notebooks and made a list:

1. Finish high school.
2. Enroll in community college.
3. Care for my baby.
4. Get married.

I stared at the last item, and my heart ached. From the time Robbie broke up with me, I had convinced myself I would never find a good guy, and I definitely would never find someone to love me *and* my child. Who would want to date a girl with a kid?

Something inside told me to pray, yet I hesitated. Was that possible? Was there really a guy out there like that? Did God hear my prayers?

There was only one way to find out.

Lord, if someone is out there, please show me, I reluctantly prayed. *I don't want the type of guy I've dated before. I want someone who loves You and who will love me and my baby with Your love. Lord, help me to trust.*

I also prayed for him—the mystery man—whoever he was. Wherever he was. The more I prayed, the more I trusted that God would answer my prayer. Desiring to pray more was the first answer to my prayers.

Prayer took my mind off my problems. After a while it wasn't the answers I was praying for. It was God Himself I wanted to be with. I was thankful and amazed that God gave me access to Him. And I trusted that He would bring about a good future. Trust was a welcome song to my heart.

> You gave me a new song,
>   a song of praise to you.
> Many will see this,
> and they will honor and trust
>   you, the LORD God.
> —Psalm 40:3 (CEV)

WHAT ABOUT YOU?

Have you ever stopped to thank God that He is with you all the time, regardless of what's happening in your life? He has made a way for us to go to Him at any time, no matter what.

In the Old Testament we read of only select people being able to go directly to God in prayer. Most used a mediator between God and them. When people wanted to communicate to God, they went to a leader, like Moses, or to the high priest. That person, in turn, would take the requests before God. God was someone to be feared, revered. The thought of having an intimate and personal relationship with Him would have been a crazy concept.

In the New Testament, the disciples saw Jesus talking to God directly. They wanted to learn to do that too. They wanted to trust that God heard them, just like Jesus trusted. They asked Jesus to teach them how to pray.

Jesus let the disciples know that they could now go directly to God and could refer to Him as their Father. Christ said, "When you pray," not "If you pray." Clearly this was to be a regular, ongoing practice.

One suggestion Jesus gave His disciples was not to babble on and on in front of people—saying empty words and trying just to look good to others. Instead He encouraged them to get away, to be alone, and to get real with God.

But when you pray, go into your room, close the door and pray to your Father, who is unseen. Then your

Father, who sees what is done in secret, will reward you.
— Matthew 6:6 (NIV)

Going to God in prayer is trusting He will make a difference. Trust means not worrying about saying the right thing. Or not feeling you have to say it over and over for God to hear. Instead it's whispering to God your darkest secrets and greatest disappointments. It's also sharing your worries— whether that worry is trusting someone with your rope or with your heart. Trust also means believing your prayers will work in the life of your future husband even though you can't see him today.

The amazing thing about prayer is that God has designed this system to release the power of heaven for the person or situation we're praying for. Think of your prayers as the garage door opener that lifts heaven's gates and sends reinforcements to strengthen your future husband.

You have most likely not met him yet, but your prayers will make a difference in his life. As you pray, you too are changed. You're building your trust. You're placing your hopes in God's hands, and there's no better place they can be.

There is no better habit than a habit of prayer.

So this is my prayer: that your love will flourish and that you will not only love much but well. Learn to love appropriately. You need to use your head and test your feelings so that your love is sincere and intelligent, not sentimental gush. Live a lover's life, circumspect and

exemplary, a life Jesus will be proud of: bountiful in
fruits from the soul, making Jesus Christ attractive to
all, getting everyone involved in the glory and praise of
God.

—Philippians 1:9–11 (MSG)

SHE PRAYED...GOD ANSWERED

I spent two years dating the wrong man before I got
together with my husband. No tragic story or anything.
The first guy just was not a good match for me. I remember praying, "Lord, I am not good at this—I will be happy
to remain single if that's what You want. I trust You. So
if You would like me to marry, please choose him for me
and let me know loud and clear."

God gave me so much more than I ever dreamed; ten
years later, and I am still amazed. —Andrea

Depend on the LORD;
    trust him, and he will take care of you.
    —Psalm 37:5 (NCV)

Every evening I turn my worries over
to God. He's going to be up all night
anyway.

—MARY C. CROWLEY

Are you worried? Sometimes you may not realize you are. Unfortunately worry can trigger your actions even when you aren't aware that it is happening. Maybe you have been striving for a boyfriend because you're worried that you'll be alone, or that others will make fun of you, or that you're unlovable. Worry is the opposite of trust.

Take out a piece of paper, and write out all those worries. Don't filter your thoughts, but instead just write them down as they come to you. Your list may look something like this:

- I'm worried I'll be the only one at school who has never gone on a date.
- I'm worried because I'm not outgoing enough to get a guy's attention.
- I'm worried that I'll end up with a loser if I don't strive for someone better.
- I'm worried that because of the mistakes I've made there won't be someone for me.

Now, take your list and hold it before God. Read over those things, and consider what Jesus would say if you could see Him by your side and hear Him. What does He want you to do? He wants you to trust.

This is what I think God would say to you:

Trust Me, Beautiful One. At the right time you will go on a date with the right person…and before then I will be here to love you and cherish you.

Trust Me, One I Love. You don't need to worry about getting the attention of someone special. Trust Me. Become the person I want you to be.

Trust Me, Woman of Worth. You don't need to strive. I have a good plan, a beautiful plan.

Trust Me, Shining Beauty. I have washed your mistakes away. I see you as beautiful and pure. I have someone in mind for you— your future husband who will see you the same way.

A Prayer for My Future Husband

Lord, right now I pray for my future husband. I can't see him, I don't know him, but I trust You hold him close to your heart. I thank You that You love him and watch over him and that some-day I can join You in doing that.

Lord, I pray my prayers will open heaven's gates and send down Your strength to him today. I pray he will learn to trust You as he never has before. I pray he will turn to You in prayer, trusting You to make a difference. I pray he will also trust that I'm out here, waiting for him. I pray these things in Your Son's name, amen.

A Prayer for Me

Dear Heavenly Father, for so long I've worried about finding the right person. I've worried I'll never have someone to love me. I've worried I'll be left out. I've feared I'll be alone. Sometimes those worries have led me to bad decisions. Always those worries have taken my mind and heart off Your plans for me and put my at-tention on the present situation. Forgive me, Lord Jesus, for my worries. Forgive me for all the desperate acts they have led me to. Your Word says that perfect love drives out fear. I want to know that type of love. Help me to realize Your love for me in ways I've never known before. Help me to trust.

I know, Lord, that many of my motives for these prayers have been about my future husband, but I also thank You that I'm changed in the process. I know that the closer I am to You, the better prepared I am for a relationship with my future husband. I know the more I depend on You, the better bond You can build with me and eventually with my husband and me. I thank You, even now, that You'll be the third strand in our relationship.

Until the right time when my future husband comes, I want You to have my whole heart, Jesus. I know that only Your love is perfect. I trust that. Amen.

Get into the habit of dealing with God about everything. Unless in the first waking moment of the day you
learn to fling the door wide back and let God in, you
will work on a wrong level all day; but swing the door
wide open and pray to your Father in secret, and every
public thing will be stamped with the presence of God.

—Oswald Chambers

My Thoughts ON MY FUTURE HUSBAND
AND ME TRUSTING

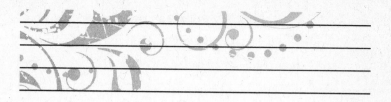

Discussion Questions

1. In what way has praying for your future husband brought you closer to God?

2. Robin talked about not being able to trust her instructor when it came to rappelling. Do you struggle with not trusting people? How does this distrust hurt your relationship with God?

3. Robin said, "In choosing to trust, I was opening myself up to all the possibilities God might have designed for me, including falling in love again." How does trusting God and trusting others prepare you for the future God has for you?

4. Read Proverbs 3:5–6. In what ways do you lean on your own understanding instead of trusting in God? How could you change that?

5. Tricia's life was changed when a group of women from church reached out to her. How has the love and care of others pointed you to God?

6. Do you worry that because of your past mistakes there won't be a good guy interested in loving you? How can praying for your future husband make a difference, even though it's hard to believe?

7. How can you change your prayer life to reflect your trust in God?

8. Read Philippians 1:9–13. What words stood out most to you? How does the world's idea of love differ from what this passage says?

9. What are some of the things that worry you as you wait for your future husband? In what ways can you turn those worries into prayers?

7

Pray for Loyalty and Faithfulness

You are always loyal
to your loyal people,
and you are faithful
to the faithful.

—Psalm 18:25 (CEV)

Robin:

For the past sixteen years I've participated in an enriching experience. Each week I meet with two very special women, and the three of us pray. When we started to meet, we agreed not to make it a social event. I was pretty bossy about what I thought our prayer time should look like.

"Don't bother to make coffee," I told Cindy and Carrie. "I don't think we need muffins to get our prayer time going. And to be honest, I don't care if your Aunt Susie is having gall bladder flareups. I just want to pray for you, your husband, and your children."

Amazingly, both of them agreed to those terms for our prayer time. We all saw it as sacred space carved out of our busy weeks; the time was a standing appointment to join hearts and get to work doing battle in the spiritual realm for our husbands and children.

We have seen God accomplish amazing things over the years. All three of us have friends we meet with for lunch and shopping, but our trio has a unique and strong relationship. We feel anchored to each other through the consistent, focused time of prayer we've shared all these years. This loyalty and faithfulness has deepened our relationships more than we could have imagined.

One simple request we made for our children early on was, "Lord, when they sin, let them get caught right away."

It's an odd request. None of us presumed our kids were faultless. We knew they would make poor choices. Everyone does. But we prayed that they would immediately be found out so that they would suffer the consequences for their wrongdoing and not hide their choices. We didn't want them to think they could develop a life pattern of getting away with sin.

As we prayed this for our children and as they got caught, we found that they were developing a stronger loyalty to the things of God. Any child who disobeys and is punished thinks twice about repeating the same disobedient act when the consequences are considered. A sense of security and confidence developed in their relationships with the Lord. They experienced the fruitful reward of loyalty and faithfulness.

What do you think about praying the same for your future husband? This is a powerful and usually overlooked prayer that could have a radical, life-changing effect on your future husband. If he is caught right away every time he gives in to temptation, he will be released from the trap the enemy has set for him. That trap is the lie that says, "Go ahead. No one will ever find out. You can do this thing that you know isn't right, and you can get away with it."

By getting caught, having an opportunity to repent, and then being restored, a young man has the chance to grow in discipline and maturity. That maturity breeds loyalty to the Lord and a life of faithfulness.

Pray that your future husband will develop a deep sense of loyalty and faithfulness.

Now Tricia has a few things to say about the irresistible attraction that grows when a man enters your life as a faithful friend.

> Never let loyalty and kindness leave you! Tie them around your neck as a reminder. Write them deep within your heart.
>
> —PROVERBS 3:3 (NLT)

Tricia:

After I dedicated my heart to Christ, I started to attend church. I also read God's Word and prayed more and more. I came to understand that Jesus was a faithful friend who would never leave me and never turn His back on me. I fell in love with Him.

I went home from the hospital the same day Cory was born, and that evening John Goyer came for a visit. Not John Goyer, my pastor, but John Goyer Jr., his son—the handsome twenty-two-year-old drummer from church.

John entered with a soft, yellow teddy bear, a card, and a big smile. "Congratulations," he said, handing the card and teddy bear to me.

"Thank you. How sweet."

I opened the card and read it. *If you need anything, let me know.* John signed it *Your friend, John.*

If I need anything? How about a husband? How about a daddy for my son? I didn't say the words, but I thought them. We chatted, and I was grateful for the new friendship. I was thankful that someone out there thought about me, cared about how I was doing.

The more I got to know John, the more I respected him. He was loyal. He was at church every week. He helped his mom and dad. He volunteered by helping with children's church. And he was faithful. He did what he said he would do. I liked that.

Soon the friendship turned into something more. A couple of weeks later my mom said, "So, I was talking to John's mom, Darlyne, and she wondered if you would go on a date with John if he asked."

I told my mom I would. He seemed like a great guy. My mom must have spread the news to Darlyne, and Darlyne must have told John, because just a few days later he called.

"Hi, Tricia. I was wondering if you would be interested in going to dinner and a movie sometime."

"Sure, uh, but I have to bring Cory since I'm nursing."

"Of course, I expected that."

When the night arrived, dinner and the movie were great. It was a little awkward having Cory there. Everyone thought he was *our* son. It was also awkward interrupting our date to go to the bathroom to breast-feed. This wasn't how first dates were supposed to be at seventeen years old.

As we sat in the movie theater, I realized not only was this my first date with John, but it also was my first real date other than the prom. The other guys I had dated hadn't treated me so well. I had never been able to talk to them as easily as I could with John. Having just ended his service with the Marine Corps, John was well traveled, mature, and interesting.

Also, John respected me, which I never had experienced with other guys. He opened doors for me. He listened as I talked. He paid for our date, and at the movie theater, he asked if he could hold my hand. After I said yes and he took my hand into his, a thousand tingles went up my arm. Even though this was our first date, his loyalty in other areas of his life gave me a glimpse into how he would treat me.

In the weeks to come, as I continued to date John, I realized God was changing my dreams. I had thought I knew the type of guy I wanted, but that wasn't the right kind of person for me.

With John, God gave me a vision of what it would be like to raise Cory in a Christian home. I liked that thought, and I had been praying for that—for a husband who would be a good example for my son and the spiritual leader in our home. Maybe this guy would fulfill my prayers.

The thing I didn't know for many months was that John's interest in me had started years before. On one of the few occasions I had attended church with my mom before I was pregnant, John saw me, and in his words, "I thought you were the prettiest girl I had ever seen."

After that service John asked his mom about me, but her response wasn't positive. "Stay away from her; she's trouble." At the time, she was right.

But years later John took a second look. I'm so glad he did. And what did he see? Loyalty.

He saw me at church and noticed a change. Although my pregnancy was evident, he claimed my love for Jesus was even more evident. God had transformed me. I was no longer a girl who wanted to do things her way; instead, I was trusting God with all my heart. I was getting to know the Lord personally, intimately. I was committed to God. My loyalty to the things of God made John risk his heart. And he soon asked me to be his wife.

When I said yes to John, I knew this man was a gift from God. Even though I had made many wrong choices, Jesus didn't put me on the "second rate" list. His plans for me were wonderful, beautiful. Jesus was loyal too. He was dedicated to me. I knew if I stuck with Him, He wasn't going to let me down.

I may have doubted that God could bring someone to love me—faults and all—but I discovered God gives us gifts at unexpected times in unexpected ways.

> Tearing your clothes is not enough to show you are sad;
>> let your heart be broken.
> Come back to the LORD your God,
>> because he is kind and shows mercy.
> He doesn't become angry quickly,
>> and he has great love.
>> He can change his mind about doing harm.…
> …anyone who calls on the LORD
>> will be saved.
>> —Joel 2:13, 32 (NCV)

WHAT ABOUT YOU?

How loyal are you to your friends? Can others trust you? Have you been faithful to your future husband, even if you haven't met him yet? And not just sexually faithful, but are you guarding your heart and emotions from guys who don't respect you or treat you with kindness? Being faithful involves more than our bodies; it involves every part of us, including our prayer lives.

If you have been caught up in the lie that you can get away with things that aren't God's desire for you, now is the time to repent. Confess what you have done. Make a fresh start. Let your lessons in loyalty begin today. As you grow in being faithful to the Lord and as you make it a practice to keep your heart clean and uncluttered with hidden sin, you will become irresistible to others. You will be the friend everyone trusts. These character qualities are like gold when it comes to a lifetime commitment.

Do you need to be reminded of some guidelines as you develop faithfulness in your own life? Here you go:

- Don't go too far, either physically or emotionally.
- Do wait.
- Don't get too close.
- Do trust God.
- Don't get too intimate.
- Do set up boundaries.
- Don't try to cover up your failures.
- Do confess and receive God's forgiveness.
- Don't go back to places where you stumbled before.
- Do set new patterns and behaviors.
- Don't date guys who are disrespectful.
- Do seek out guys who are faithful in all their relationships.

What about your history of making choices? Do you need to pull back from making impulsive, self-satisfying decisions when it comes to guys? Maybe you need to turn over the key to the garden of your heart to the Lord and let Him make the decisions about who can come and go from that garden.

The following poem is one that Robin wrote in her journal when she was in a season of handing over more control of her life to Christ. As her loyalty to the Lord was growing, she wanted to make sure she was being faithful and true to the dreams He had for her. A version of this poem appears in *A Promise Is Forever,* in volume 4 of the Christy Miller Series.

Within my heart a garden grows
Wild with violets and fragrant rose.
Bright daffodils line the narrow path
My footsteps silent as I pass.
Sweet tulips nod their heads in rest,
I kneel in prayer to seek God's best.
For round my garden a fence stands firm
To guard my heart so I can learn
Who should enter and who should wait
On the other side of my locked gate.
I clasp the key around my neck
And wonder if the time is yet
If I unlocked the gate today
Would he come in or run away?
I do not want to hold this key
Lord, will You keep it safe for me?
Then when he comes
If he's the one
You'll unlock the gate
Until then, I'll wait.

Robin:

The above poem was used in a sweet and unexpected way in the life of one young girl who read this series. During the twenty-five years I've been writing teen novels, I've received a lot of mail from readers. Hundreds and maybe thousands of young women have told me that they are praying for their future husbands. But last March I received a letter that especially affected me.

This four-page missive came from a tender-hearted father. Along with the letter was a program from his fifteen-year-old daughter's memorial service.

I stopped everything to read what the dad had written. "Elizabeth loved all your books. She was a walking, talking, passionate billboard for our Lord."

He went on to explain how unexpected her passing was. "The medical examiner wasn't able to determine the cause of death, but we know she is now with the One she loved more than anyone else in the world—our Lord, Jesus Christ."

I reached for the box of tissues and read on. "Elizabeth kept a journal. She wrote letters to her future husband. I have never read anything quite like it and probably never will again. Her last journal entry was a quote from one of your books: Christy Miller, vol. 4, the poem about the garden of the heart. She copied it word for word. It was probably written just before she went into Glory."

I wrote back to Elizabeth's parents, and five months later, I had an opportunity to have lunch with Elizabeth's mom and her younger sister, Jodie. Her mother offered to send me copies of the letters Elizabeth wrote to her future husband along with copies of her journal entries.

A few weeks later I sat alone by the fire reading the pages

in Elizabeth's handwriting and was captured by declarations such as:

- Right now I feel so clean, pure, and innocent. I want to always be that way until we meet.
- Purity is about keeping your heart, mind, and body pure. I want my heart to stay intact so I can give it to you. I want to give you my heart.
- On my wedding day, I long to be in a white wedding gown, walking down the aisle to my beloved with my dad on my arm. I lift my eyes behind my veil to see my True Love.

In all the ways that matter, every one of Elizabeth's wishes and requests for her future husband had come true—in heaven.

Elizabeth had faithfully prayed for her future husband, never realizing how her prayers would be answered. She was now face to face with her True Love. She was clothed in a pure white gown. She was able to present to her Prince of Peace her whole heart—clean, pure, and innocent. The reality of how her prayers had been fulfilled was sobering. Once again I saw the mystery of prayer and the bigger picture of God's unfathomable power. What remains unshaken throughout history and continues into eternity is God's deep, unfailing, and ever-faithful love toward us. To trust an inexplicable God with complete abandonment is an act of true faith. And to the faithful, He shows Himself faithful.

I am my beloved's and my beloved is mine.
—Song of Solomon 6:3 (NASB)

How Do I Pray That My Future Husband Is Loyal and Faithful?

- Pray that he gets caught when he does wrong.
- Pray that he will be released from the enemy's trap of believing he can hide his sin.
- Pray that God will give him good examples of couples who have remained faithful throughout their marriage.
- Pray that he will be given opportunities to make choices that cause him to demonstrate his loyalty and faithfulness to his friends and family.

She Prayed...God Answered

I prayed for my future husband from middle school on. I really wanted him to be faithful to me. I prayed that I would be loyal to him and not drawn into dating, but that I would be drawn to date the one God intended for me—and him alone. My first boyfriend was my only boyfriend, and we both saved ourselves for marriage. We've been married now for more than thirteen years, and we are more in love every day thanks to God's amazing grace. —Liz

Understand, therefore, that the LORD your God is indeed God. He is the faithful God who keeps his covenant for a thousand generations and lavishes his

unfailing love on those who love him and obey his
commands.

—Deuteronomy 7:9 (NLT)

A Prayer for My Future Husband

*Dear Gracious God, today I pray that my future husband will be
faithful to You. I pray that his heart will grow tender toward
You, Lord. I pray that when he makes wrong choices, he will get
caught. I pray that he will immediately confess to You and that
he will experience Your forgiveness and grace. Teach him how to
be faithful to his friends. Show him the attractiveness of being
loyal.*

*I pray that my future husband will trust in You with all his
heart, and he won't be distracted by what looks good or what he
figures is best. I pray that he will spend time with You and live for
You, not by following a list of rules but rather by having a personal
and intimate relationship with You. Listen to his prayers and surprise him with Your goodness. Thank You for hearing my prayers.
In Jesus' name, amen.*

A Prayer for Me

*Dear Lord God, I admit that sometimes I don't pray from deep in
my heart because I'm afraid I'll be disappointed. Right now I just
want to thank You that You care about the deepest desires of my
heart. I'm amazed that You love me more than anyone else loves me
and that You love to show me how deeply You care.*

Help me to seek You diligently with all my heart. I pray that each day I'll get to know You better. I pray that as I grow closer to You, I'll also be more sensitive to Your ways. Help me be tender to those You bring into my life.

Most of all, I pray that I will be loyal to You and not to my own desires. Help me, Lord, to be sensitive to Your plan…and to Your timing. Whenever I become eager to head off on my own path, help me remember that Your best plan also comes at Your appointed time. In Jesus' name, amen.

The LORD must wait for you to come to him
   so he can show you his love and compassion.
For the LORD is a faithful God.
   —Isaiah 30:18 (NLT)

My Thoughts ON MY FUTURE HUSBAND AND ME BEING LOYAL AND FAITHFUL

Discussion Questions

1. Robin talked about praying for her kids, *Lord, if they do something wrong, help them to get caught right away.* What do you think about that prayer?

2. Have you ever considered praying that your future husband would get caught right away when he does something wrong? Would that prayer help him or hurt him?

3. What would you think if your future husband were praying that for you?

4. Tricia talked about meeting John and noticing how loyal he was—to his work, to church, to family, and to friends. Why does the degree of loyalty in a guy's life now reflect the level of loyalty he will have as a husband?

5. Had you thought of loyalty and faithfulness as important qualities to look for in a future husband? In what ways has this chapter adjusted your thinking?

6. Like Robin and Tricia, you might discover that God's ideas and your ideas for your future differ. How do you feel about praying, *Lord, I want You to choose*?

7. In what areas of your life do you need to be more loyal?

8. Why does being faithful to the Lord make us irresistible to others?

9. What lines in Robin's poem stand out the most to you? Why?

10. Can you think of examples of couples you know who have been loyal and faithful in their marriages? What do you appreciate most about them?

11. In what ways has God been faithful to you? How does this past faithfulness encourage you while you're waiting for your future husband?

8

Pray

for Strength

I love you, LORD; you are my strength.

—PSALM 18:1 (NLT)

Robin:

When you hear the word *strength* connected to your future husband, you immediately think of muscles, right? Muscles are a very nice feature in a husband. They come in handy when you decide to rearrange the furniture or need help to open a jar. But strength comes in a variety of forms:

- strength of character
- strength of spirit
- strength in leadership
- strength to resist temptation
- strength in reputation

I'm sure you can think of a few more. Go ahead and list them. (It's okay to write in this book.)

_____

_____

_____

My husband most definitely had strength of presence when I first met him. And let me just say we did not get off on the best foot.

I was a freshman in college, and every week I taught a junior high Sunday school class. The youth pastor asked if I would help out on a four-day bike ride over Easter vacation. I agreed to go, happy to have something to do over the break.

We pedaled through rain on the first day and had to spend the night on the hard floor of a musty old church. Early the next morning, while the thunder and lightning were going at it outside, someone pounded on the door of the fellowship hall. I was alone with the girls while the boys were sleeping at the other end of the church with the youth pastor. The girls squealed when they heard a man's voice yell, "Hey, open the door!"

I went to the locked door and bravely yelled, "Who is it?"

"Ross Gunn. Open the door! We're getting soaked out here."

I knew another youth leader was arriving a day late with one of the junior high boys, but I didn't know his name.

Ross yelled one more time, "Come on! Open up!"

Reluctantly, I opened the door only a few inches and looked into the face of my future husband for the first time. Of course, I didn't know he was my future husband. I thought he was a rather bold (and cute) guy who had a commanding strength of presence. He entered, rain soaked and irritated, and trekked toward the other end of the building with the equally soaked junior high boy right behind him.

The next time our eyes met was an hour later. The teens were gathered in the church kitchen eating breakfast rolls. Ross told them to throw away their trash and pack their gear, and they did. He was a strong, determined man, and all the kids loved him. He was a leader, and they felt safe following him.

My first thoughts about Ross weren't as favorable as the teens'. I was intimidated by his strength. And besides, I had a boyfriend. Mike and I had been dating for a few months, and his mellow temperament was more to my liking. Mike never would pound on a door or demand to be let inside out of the rain. He wouldn't take a stand or put up a fight. Mike just let things go—and in the midst of our engagement I was one of those things he let go of without a fight.

But back to the bike ride. In organizing the logistics of that day's ride, our youth pastor said that someone had to forego biking and drive Ross's car to the campsite where we would stay that night. The task fell to me. I didn't mind a bit not bicycling another day in the rain.

As soon as all the bikers were on their way, I slipped into Ross's car and waved as I passed the group and drove on to the campsite. Just then the sun came out. Suddenly the day turned glorious for a bike ride. I pulled down the visor to block the sun, and that one act changed my opinion of Ross.

On the backside of the visor was a list. I read the first few items and realized I was reading Ross's prayer list. Knowing how personal such a list could be, I stopped reading. I put the visor back up and squinted as I drove. But what I had seen on the list was now intensely burned on my thoughts. Ross's number one prayer item was "Pray for my future wife."

PRAY THAT YOUR FUTURE HUSBAND WILL BE A STRONG PRAYER WARRIOR

Clearly Ross had deep inner strength in the spiritual area of his life. I never had met a guy who said he was praying for his future wife. I thought I was the only one doing that, as I wrote letters and prayed for my future mate.

But I didn't take the time to learn anything else about Ross during that bike ride. I was too twitterpated over Mike to see that inner, spiritual strength is a hidden treasure in a man. My view of guys during my early college years was focused a little too much on the outside and not as much on the inside. I even told my sister that I was positive I would marry a man who had dark, curly hair. She told me, "You marry the heart, not the hair."

And she was right.

Tricia didn't have a sister giving her insights while she was dating John. She did have a revealing conversation, however, that opened her eyes to what inner strength looks like in a man who is honoring God with his life.

And you must love the LORD your
God with all your heart, all your
soul, and all your strength.

—DEUTERONOMY 6:5 (NLT)

Tricia:

When a couple starts to date, it's only natural to wonder about the person's past relationships. Obviously I had been in at least one relationship before because I had a son, but I wanted to know about John. Had he dated much? Had he fallen in love before?

"Tell me about your first girlfriend," I asked on one of our dates.

"Well, she was a girl my brother's wife knew. She was cute and nice, but we didn't date long."

"Really? Why?" I asked.

"After we started to date, I battled what I wanted in the immediate—a girlfriend—with what I wanted in my future—a godly Christian wife. I wasn't sure if this girl was the one God wanted for me, so I prayed. After prayer, I knew she wasn't the one, so I broke up."

"Was it hard to break up?" I asked, my eyes fixed on his. The guys I had dated never talked like this. They never discussed seeking God's will or their thoughts of a future wife.

"Actually, it wasn't hard," John said. "I prayed that, if this wasn't the one for me, God would take away my feelings for her.

God answered that prayer, and those emotions were gone. I felt bad for her, but I knew I was doing the right thing."

As John told me that, I was amazed by his strength. First of all, I was awed that he wanted to seek God's will for his life. Second, that he was willing to pray that prayer. And third, that he followed through.

The more I got to know John, the more I realized his strength carried him through many other challenging times. He had been through a few dating relationships but always was quick to seek God and discern God's will. After high school John went into the Marine Corps. As you might guess, the military isn't an easy place to keep high standards. John would walk out of groups when they started filthy talk. He stayed away from the beaches and clubs that lonely soldiers were drawn to.

Once, while his unit was staying overnight in the Philippines, a knock sounded on his door. Opening it, he found the hotel manager there with a prostitute. John was far from home, and surely no one would know if he invited her in. But instead of falling to temptation, John paid for the man to send her home for the night—to her own home. I was amazed when I heard this story. Not only because of the strength John possessed, but because of the man he was. He had stood against temptation in this area—and others—and walked away stronger for it.

I knew this was the type of man I wanted to spend my life with.

Have I not commanded you? Be strong and courageous. Do not be afraid; do not be discouraged,
for the LORD your God will be with you wherever
you go.
    —Joshua 1:9 (NIV)

WHAT ABOUT YOU?

Think about the men you admire. That might be your dad, an
older brother, a teacher at school, a pastor, or a leader in your
community. Take a moment to write down a list of qualities
you admire about him.

Character traits:

Spiritual strengths:

Ways he holds out against temptation:

Making a list of qualities you appreciate in others is a great
way to prepare yourself to be watchful for those things in guys.
In both of our cases, our hearts had first been drawn to other
men for various reasons, but the strength of our future husbands captivated us in the end.

How Do I Pray That My Future Husband Will Be Strong?

- Pray he will be surrounded by God-Lover friends who will set the standard.
- Pray he will develop discipline in his prayer life and consistently read God's Word.
- Pray he will have a long vision to look to the future instead of focusing on present desires.
- Pray he will stand firm against the forces of evil in our culture.

She Prayed…God Answered

I prayed for my future husband after I started to read the Christy Miller books. Little did I know my fifteen-year-old high school boyfriend would grow up with me and become that man. I get overwhelmed when I think about how I prayed for Ricky at the same time I was praying for my future husband. God faithfully grew us into the man and woman He planned for us to be individually and as husband and wife. —Anna

While I was dating my boyfriend, he seemed like the perfect one for me, and I was smitten. Several months into our relationship, I noticed red flags. I knew they were warning signs, but I didn't want to be a quitter—

I didn't want to give up. I thought if I stayed in the relationship, it would work out. I just needed to be strong. For two years I prayed that God wouldn't take my boyfriend away from me. I poured all of me—mind, heart, soul…and, finally, body—into this relationship, trying desperately to convince myself that he was "The One." When I thought I was weeks away from an engagement ring and months away from a wedding day, my boyfriend ended our relationship. I remember driving home and sobbing. I couldn't stop asking God why it was ending this way. I had prayed so much, and I had searched after God's will, but I hadn't listened years earlier when God told me to let go. It took awhile, but as I began to heal, I realized that just because I prayed my boyfriend would be "The One," it didn't mean he was right for me. Now I've begun to pray for my true future husband…and I'm praying that God will prepare me for him too so that I'll have the strength to do everything I'm asking God to help my future husband to do.
—Aimee

Search for the LORD
and for his strength;
continually seek him.

—1 CHRONICLES 16:11 (NLT)

A Prayer for My Future Husband

Dear Lord, in a world that marvels at guys who are handsome and physically strong, I pray that the gift You impart most to my future husband is an inner spiritual strength. I pray that this strength will grow as he turns to You in times of difficulty or temptation. I pray that in whatever areas he is weak, he will ask You in prayer to make him strong.

Lord, I pray his strength will make him into a leader who can guide our home. I pray he will stand up against the fleeting temptations this world offers. I pray he will connect with friends who will encourage his strength instead of pulling him down. Just as weights and repetition build muscle mass, I pray the world's burdens and the daily trials will work for his good, not harm. In Jesus' name, amen.

A Prayer for Me

Lord, just as I pray for strength for my future husband, I pray the same for me. When my feelings pull me toward a certain young man, I pray I'll turn to You first, instead of entertaining those thoughts and letting my imagination run wild. I pray that as I get on my knees, You will make me strong. I pray that I will not become weary in praying for my future husband but rather that I'll be diligent at this task, knowing he will benefit and I will too.

And, Lord, each day something seems to weigh me down. I believe what Your Word says in Nehemiah 8:10—that the joy of the Lord is my strength. Please fill me with Your joy, Lord. Help me remember that strength comes when I turn to You, and You empower me for my tasks. I pray for that now. In Jesus' name, amen.

> Each time he said, "My grace is all you need. My power works best in weakness." So now I am glad to boast about my weaknesses, so that the power of Christ can work through me.
> —2 Corinthians 12:9 (NLT)

My Thoughts ON MY FUTURE HUSBAND AND ME BEING STRONG

DISCUSSION QUESTIONS

1. Look over the following list. Which of these qualities matters most to you? Why?
   - strength of character
   - strength of spirit

- strength in leadership
- strength to resist temptation
- strength in reputation

2. How would you feel if you knew your future husband
   was praying for you? What things would you like him
   to pray about?

3. Read 1 Samuel 16:7. What does God see when He
   looks at your heart?

4. What do you hope God sees when He looks at your
   future husband's heart?

5. Robin talked about being intimidated by Ross's
   strength of presence, yet that quality helped to balance
   out Robin. What qualities in your future husband do
   you think would help to balance out you?

6. What specific temptations might your future husband
   be facing today? How can you pray for his strength?

7. How do godly friends help us to be strong? Share a specific time a godly friend helped to strengthen you.

8. Just as weights and repetition build muscle mass, how can the world's burdens and the daily trials work for your future husband's good, not harm?

9. Read 2 Corinthians 12:9. How does this verse speak to your heart? How do your weaknesses allow God to be strong?

Pray

for Protection

God's way is perfect.
All the LORD's promises prove true.
He is a shield for all who look to him
for protection.

—2 SAMUEL 22:31 (NLT)

Robin:

Tricia and I believe the prayers offered from the heart of a righteous young woman can actually protect her future husband's heart and life.

Why do we believe such a mysterious thing? Because that's what Jesus prayed for us. Did you catch that? Jesus prayed for us.

On the night He was betrayed, Jesus met in an upper room with His twelve closest friends and said, "I am praying not only for these disciples but also for all who will ever believe in me through their message" (John 17:20, NLT). The "all who will ever believe" is us. We have come to believe in Christ—in His death, resurrection, and power to give us everlasting life.

Imagine: Jesus was about to be captured, beaten, and crucified; yet He prayed for *us*. Such incredible love!

What did Jesus pray? He prayed for our protection: "My prayer is not that you take them out of the world but that you protect them from the evil one" (verse 15, NIV).

Pray that your future husband will be protected from the evil one.

A realm that we can't see is in motion every moment of our lives. Angels? Demons? Evil spirits? They are all real and very much at war in the spiritual realm. As a daughter of the King of this universe, you are equipped with everything you need to fight for your future husband in this battle.

God has even described in Ephesians 6:10–18 the stunning outfit His warrior women are to put on as they go to war. He follows the wardrobe description with this line: "Be alert and always keep on praying" (verse 18, NIV). Prayer is our secret weapon. Prayer infiltrates the enemy's encampment and sends the evil one running. Prayer releases the power of God's Spirit and sends His angels to fight in the invisible realm.

The Bible has lots of amazing accounts of how God sent His angels to protect His children. One of my favorites is when Elisha and his servant woke to find their city surrounded by the invading army of Aram. The servant was understandably terrified. "What shall we do?"

"Don't be afraid," Elisha told him. "Those who are with us are more than those who are with them."

I'm sure this declaration of confidence made no sense to the young man, because all he could see was Elisha and he as the "us" and a vast army with horses and chariots as the "them."

Then (I love this part!) Elisha prayed, "O LORD, open his eyes," and the Lord did. He opened the spiritual eyes of the servant so he could see the "us" who were about to fight the battle. The hills were covered with what is described as "chariots of fire." Elisha and his servant plus God's army far outnumbered the enemy.

The Lord protected His people that day in a unique way. You can read the whole story in 2 Kings 6.

The amazing part about being in God's eternal kingdom is that those chariots of fire haven't rusted or gone out of service. They still are ready at God's command to come to our aid. One pure-hearted, praying woman *plus* the host of heaven's armies will always outnumber the troops of the evil one.

> But the Lord is faithful, and he will strengthen you and protect you from the evil one.
>
> —2 THESSALONIANS 3:3 (NIV)

I distinctly remember praying for Ross's protection soon after we began dating. He was a bit of a risktaker, more than most guys I had known, and he was definitely a warrior at heart. I was attracted to those qualities in him when our paths crossed again two years after we first met on the bike ride. I liked the fighting spirit I was getting to know in this brave-hearted Scotsman.

Our reconnection happened through a mutual friend, and our first date sparked a surprisingly easy friendship. As we dated, our friendship grew steadily into an abiding sort of love. I quickly realized that if I was going to keep up with this man on a tandem life journey, I needed to learn how to pray like a daughter of the King.

Ross prayed all the time. I mean, all the time. Prayer was and still is like breathing for him. The conversation he had with God was ongoing all day, every day. Not only did he faithfully pray for the people on the list I had spotted on his car's visor years earlier, but he also prayed for things as basic as a parking spot in a crowded lot.

God answered his prayers. I saw it happen every time I was with him. His prayers unleashed supernatural power.

I soon saw that men like Ross, who take a firm stand for the Lord, come under attack from the evil one in ways that aren't always obvious. And the attack is ongoing. If I was to commit myself to Ross in the covenant relationship of marriage, I knew that I needed to pray every day for protection for this man.

At the same time, I knew that marrying him would be the most natural next step in our relationship and in my life. The ease of that decision surprised me. You know how people tell you that "when you know, you know"? Well, it's true. When you're becoming knit together at the heart level and when you're both growing closer to God, the choice to marry is a peace-giving small step.

It's funny how the picture of this step of commitment is so different in film and on television from the way it is in real life. It's not a stressful nail-biter, wondering if you'll be asked or whether you'll accept this rose. Nor is the decision to marry this person a huge leap accompanied by the fear of loss or angst over the future. The proposal isn't a surprise. It doesn't warrant a yes or no answer because the next step is obvious to both people. Most often the response to the question, "Will you marry me?" is simply, "Of course." A relationship protected through prayer is marked by the many small steps the couple takes together all the way to the altar. Their path is made straight. Their hearts are fixed on Him. And there is peace.

> Spread your protection over them,
> > that those who love your name may rejoice in you.
> —Psalm 5:11 (NIV)

Tricia:

Many things could have crushed John before we got together. He was in the Marine Corps, stationed aboard a navy ship, and found himself in dangerous waters. He faced spiritual challenges and emotional challenges. Even physical ones.

Two years into his six-year military commitment, John was a passenger in a truck that hit a tree. That was the end of his military career and almost the end of his life.

After the accident, John had many injuries. While I was living my high school years focused on whom I wanted to date and when, John was in a body cast with a broken back, experiencing horrible pain.

His body healed, and I turned from my wayward ways. That's when God brought our paths together.

Before I knew John, God had protected him from much; but once we started to date, I realized the thing John needed the most protection from was a broken heart.

You see, as is often the case, once John and I began to date, I became desirable to the guys who had dumped me. Now that they could no longer have me, they were interested. Even my son's biological father tested the waters a few times, just to see if he still had a chance. At other times old boyfriends seemed to materialize out of nowhere.

I would be lying to say I wasn't tempted, especially by Robbie. All the emotions I had wrapped up in him were still there. Even though he was bad news, I wanted him to want me. And I know it sounds crazy, but sometimes when I pondered too long on the past, I remembered only the good times Robbie and I had together, while forgetting the bad.

During this time of dating John, I prayed for his protection. I did this by asking God to change my heart. I wanted to commit myself to this wonderful, godly man God had given to me as a gift. John trusted me. He was willing to take a chance by giving me his heart. I knew that flirting with those old temptations would bring pain to the man I was growing to love.

Many things can hurt a man, but nothing hurts him worse than the woman he loves casting her thoughts and eyes toward another. As John and I grew closer and soon became engaged, I felt the battle waging within.

Sometimes, you see, the enemy uses things "out there" to hurt the ones we love. Other times he uses our sinful nature to battle our spirit within. We end up being the source of hurt. The apostle Paul wrote about this in Romans 7:15, 17–18 (NIV):

> I do not understand what I do. For what I want to do I
> do not do, but what I hate I do.... As it is, it is no longer
> I myself who do it, but it is sin living in me. For I know
> that good itself does not dwell in me, that is, in my
> sinful nature.

As you go through life, you may find your biggest battle is within. You do the things you don't want to do. You don't do the things you should. This is something you need to pray about now, today. Strength for your husband to battle his sinful nature is something you need to pray for him too.

One prayer I pray often is Psalm 139:23–24 (AMP):

> Search me [thoroughly], O God, and know my heart!
> Try me and know my thoughts! And see if there is any
> wicked or hurtful way in me, and lead me in the way
> everlasting.

It's too easy for us to walk through life and act as though we have everything together while rottenness is growing inside. How much better to live each day knowing your heart and thoughts are blameless before God because you've sought Him and asked Him to make you clean. All of us need forgiveness—and cleansing—every day.

As the years have passed, for me the battle of temptation has flared up at different times. By giving myself away—body, emotions, heart—to others before I met John, I carried those memories deep within, the tender moments as well as the painful ones. God has continued to bring healing in this area, but it's taken a lot of prayer. John prays for me, and I pray for him. Our prayers for each other started during our dating years, and we've discovered their power through the years that followed. Prayer makes all the difference. My heart knows that well.

> May integrity and uprightness protect me,
>   because my hope, LORD, is in you.
>   —Psalm 25:21 (NIV)

WHAT ABOUT YOU?

Do you have someone who prays for you? Ask that person to pray for your protection from the evil one. Ask him or her to pray for your mind, emotions, and heart. There is no place the enemy won't try to penetrate.

In every situation, remind yourself that you belong to Christ. He lives in you. As 1 John 4:4 says, "Greater is He who is in you than he who is in the world" (NASB). Jesus has the power to win every challenge or battle you're facing today. Your job is to turn to Him, to seek Him, to pray.

HOW DO I PRAY THAT MY FUTURE HUSBAND WILL BE PROTECTED?

Pray that every day he will put on the whole armor of God, as listed in Ephesians 6, so he can stand against the evil one. Specifically pray that:

- He will put on the belt of truth around his waist. Pray he will keep that belt cinched tightly.
- He will wear the breastplate of righteousness. Making good decisions and living in a way that honors God will protect his heart the way a breastplate protects a warrior's vital organs.
- He will slip his feet into marching boots. That way he always will be ready to go where God leads him. He will be equipped to journey through difficult places to tell others the great news of how they can have peace with God.
- He will pick up the shield of faith daily. Pray he will hold that shield steady to protect him from the flaming arrows the enemy will shoot at him every day of his life.
- He will put on the helmet of salvation so that his mind will be protected with the knowledge of who he is in Christ. He is a redeemed, adopted son of

the Most High God. Pray that this identity will be
firmly in place and protect his thoughts.

- He will learn how to wield the sword of the Spirit,
  which is the Word of God. Pray that he will pull
  out that sword and use it to slice through the
  attacks of the evil one. Pray also that he will realize
  all he needs for life is found in God's Word.

Remember to pray the same—in all these ways—for
yourself.

SHE PRAYED...GOD ANSWERED

I remember once when I was seventeen feeling an urgent
burden to pray for my future husband. I prayed that
wherever he was God would protect him and be very real
to him regardless of what was happening. Years later,
when I was dating the man who is now my husband, he
told me a story that convinced me he was the man I had
prayed for.

He was at a summer pool party during which everyone was drinking. He was inebriated, but suddenly he
experienced clarity. He remembers looking at all the
drunk partygoers and feeling an overwhelming sense that
he didn't belong there. He got up and went home. After
that night he walked away from that lifestyle and those
friends and began his journey with Christ. I believe without a doubt that it was the same night I was praying for
him with such urgency. —Emily

During what turned out to be a three-month break between school and the start of my career, all I could think about was what my future held. A guy was on the top of that list. My mom suggested we spend this waiting period praying for my future husband.

She told me we would pray an hour each day, and she was serious about it. We would head to her bedroom, and I would sit on her bed or kneel. We would pray that God would be with my future husband. That God would keep him pure. We would pray for his heart and that he would be a warrior for God. My mom meant business!

We prayed seven days a week. For six days we would pray many requests for my future husband. On the seventh day, we would praise God for those requests. We would thank God for keeping him pure, for his heart, for his stand for God.

When my new career started, my prayer times with my mother ended, but I continued to pray for my future husband on my own. Three years later, a friend of a friend contacted me via instant message. He was trying to contact someone else and found me by accident, but we struck up a friendship. Turns out he was the one!

I know that my prayers made a difference. Every prayer I prayed was like a shield of protection around my future husband. Also, in the process of praying, I changed too.

I'm so glad my mom joined in those prayers with me. It reminds me of what it says in Ecclesiastes 4:9–10:

"Two are better than one, because they have a good reward for their labor. For if they fall, one will lift up his companion" [NKJV]. My life was changed forever because of those prayers. —Shannon R.

> Our God, our help in ages past,
> Our hope for years to come,
> Be Thou our guard while troubles last,
> And our eternal home.
>
> —ISAAC WATTS

A Prayer for My Future Husband

Dear Lord, wherever my future husband is at this moment, I pray for his protection. I pray You place a camp of angels around him. I pray You keep Your ear perked to his cries for help, and in the battles he faces, I pray You will open his eyes to see that Your forces are standing against the enemy.

I pray my future husband will put on Your armor each day. I pray he will understand the difference in a day that he dresses for the battle versus the day he feels too lazy or forgets.

I pray that You will help him to fight not only the outward forces that try to bring him down but also the sin nature inside. Sometimes, Lord, our greatest battles are with our own sinful, fleshly wants. I pray You will help him be strong in this area too.

And finally, Lord, I thank You for all the ways You already have protected him—ways we may not know until we enter eternity with You. Thank You, thank You, thank You! Amen.

A PRAYER FOR ME

Dear Lord, I know my weaknesses better than anyone. I understand how I've hurt others. How I've been unkind. How I'm drawn to things that hurt me and how I turn my back on things that are good. I pray for my own protection, Lord. I pray You will protect me from harm and from myself. I understand, Lord, that the decisions I make will protect my future husband from having his heart broken by me.

Each day, Lord, remind me to dress myself for battle. I need my heart shielded, my mind protected, truth tied tight around me, my feet prepared to step out to do Your work, faith as my shield, and Your Spirit as my sword. I pray these things in Jesus' name, amen.

> "Because he loves me," says the LORD,
> "I will rescue him;
> I will protect him, for he acknowledges my name."
> —Psalm 91:14 (NIV)

My Thoughts ON MY FUTURE HUSBAND AND ME BEING PROTECTED

DISCUSSION QUESTIONS

1. How does it make you feel to know that the night before Jesus died on the cross He was praying for your protection?

2. Jesus prayed that we would be protected from the evil one. What helps you to remember that someone is setting out to bring you down?

3. Recall a time when God opened your eyes to see His power and protection around you.

4. What prayers of protection can you pray specifically for your future husband?

5. Tricia talked about her emotions over past relationships

being something that hurt John's heart. When old emotions crop up for you, how can you protect yourself from them?

6. Read Romans 7:15–25. As you go through life, you may also find your biggest battle is within. What battles can your friends join you in praying about?

7. In what ways do integrity and uprightness protect us, as Psalm 25:21 says? How can you apply that verse to praying for your future husband?

8. In what ways does it take courage to pray Psalm 139:23–24 (AMP): "Search me [thoroughly], O God, and know my heart! Try me and know my thoughts! And see if there is any wicked or hurtful way in me, and lead me in the way everlasting"?

9. Why do you think the wardrobe list for a woman fighting for spiritual triumph in Ephesians 6 ends with: "Be alert and always keep on praying" (verse 18, NIV)?

10

Pray for Intimacy

There's more to sex than mere skin on skin.
Sex is as much spiritual mystery as physical fact.
As written in Scripture,
"The two become one."…
We must not pursue the kind of sex
that avoids commitment and intimacy,
leaving us more lonely than ever—
the kind of sex that can never "become one."

—1 Corinthians 6:16–18 (msg)

Robin:

Here it is—the chapter in which we get to talk about your future husband being a good lover as well as a God Lover.

Sexual intimacy with our spouse is only one kind of intimacy. We all experience intimate relationships that aren't sexual, including our relationship with the Lord. The first image that comes to mind when I think of a God Lover demonstrating intimacy toward the Lord is the picture described for us at the Last Supper when John laid his head on Christ's chest. John's relationship with the Lord was so close that he had the freedom to express himself to his Savior in an extraordinary, unguarded manner.

Isn't it amazing that we are offered that same intimate closeness with the Lord when we come to Him in prayer? He made it possible for us to draw that close and to speak with Him that confidently.

The same night of the Last Supper, Jesus explained to His disciples that the relationship between God and us was about to change. Jesus said we were no longer to see ourselves as servants or slaves, trying to live out every detail of the law so we could draw close to God. He explained that "a master doesn't confide in his slaves." Then Jesus told the disciples, "Now you are my friends" (John 15:15, NLT).

When true friendship begins between two people, everything changes. Friendship is the quiet, first step to intimacy. And just imagine: We are invited to become friends with the Son of God. He confides in His friends. We draw close and share our deepest thoughts and feelings with Him. This is where a God Lover learns the meaning of intimacy.

Intimacy happens at the heart level and affects how you think about yourself and your future husband—not just his body but also his soul and spirit. Intimacy creates confidence. When this sort of openness and assurance is in place early in a friendship, you know that all you have shared with the other person will be respected, valued, and honored.

We don't seem to have a lot of examples in the stories shown in movies or on television of what this sort of invisible bonding looks like. It's easy to find images of what physical intimacy looks like, but what's missing is the real-life ingredient of true intimacy at the heart level.

Every human is made up of three key components:

- spirit—the invisible part of us that lives forever; the heart or core of us
- soul—our mind, emotions, and will
- body—the physical

Real intimacy meshes all three of these areas. God's intent for a man and woman in marriage is that a bond as strong as Super Glue will form between them. Sounds easy, but it's not. Why is that?·

I think this bond of intimacy became a fragile thing all the way back in the Garden of Eden with Adam and Eve. God made one man and one woman, and He designed them to be joined together. This is still His design: one woman, one man for life. Before the Fall, Adam and Eve had nothing to hide from each other, and Scripture tells us, "Adam and his wife were both naked, and they felt no shame" (Genesis 2:25, NIV).

True intimacy feels no shame. You can entrust to your spouse all that you are—spirit, soul, and body—and know that you will be heard, seen, accepted, and understood.

Remember what happened after the Fall? The first thing Adam and Eve did was stitch fig leaves together in an effort to cover up their bodies from each other. Then they withdrew from walking around openly in the garden and tried to hide from God. Their intimacy with God was broken as well as their intimacy with each other.

Marriage allows us a chance to experience in a volatile, fragile way the original intimacy that was intended between a man and his wife when God created them to be naked and not ashamed. Any woman who has experienced this will tell you what an incredibly beautiful and surprisingly powerful thing it is to appear naked before only one man in your life and, because of the bond of the marriage covenant, to do so feeling no shame. But it's not just the freedom to be unabashedly naked that nurtures intimacy. It's the freedom to offer to your spouse all that you are in spirit, soul, and body and to know that you will be accepted, honored, and loved.

Intimacy expresses itself in knowing looks shared across the room, in a tender touch at just the right moment, and by whispered words of affection.

When a husband and wife come together in unguarded intimacy, their relationship deepens over the years, and each of them finds that his or her thoughts, feelings, and body—those precious attributes that previously had been hidden—can be shared with this other person. Part of the sacredness of marriage is entering this safe haven where everything about you can be offered openly without shame.

I remember the first really horrible fight Ross and I had after we were married. It started with a conversation during which both of us seemed to go to a deeper level of vulnerability. Our exchange included blatant honesty, tears, yelling, silence, forgiveness, more tears, and finally a deep and settling peace.

I went to bed that night feeling so intimately connected to my husband because I knew we were in this relationship for the long journey. Neither of us had anything to hide. Even when the worst came out in both of us, we could work through it. I found that I could entrust to him the deepest, ugliest parts of my heart, and in the process, our intimacy would grow stronger.

One of God's intentions for marriage is that it last a lifetime so that intimacy would be given the time and space it needs to knit two people together at the heart level. Why is that important? This sort of intimacy with another person gives us a clearer understanding of the depth of intimacy God wants us to have in our relationship with Him. He wants us to draw closer and closer to Him. He wants for us the same thing He wanted for Adam and Eve—to come out of hiding, to be open and honest before Him, and to go the distance in our relationship with Him. Each step that brings us closer to God brings us into a more intimate and peaceful relationship with Him.

Intimacy is a fine and delicate gift. God designed this gift to be shared between one man and one woman for a lifetime so that they might be naked before each other spiritually, emotionally, and physically and not be ashamed.

Pray that your future husband will guard his spirit, soul, and body so that the two of you might fully experience the gift of intimacy.

When Ross and I became engaged, like all young couples in love, we couldn't wait to get married. We kept discovering how well our opposite ways of thinking and doing things balanced each other. We each started to align our life to fit into the other's. Our minds, emotions, and desires meshed together so nicely. It felt torturous not to be able to explore how our bodies would fit together.

But we knew the reward would be great if we waited.

To solidify our agreement to wait, we bought a greeting card and a picture frame. The card had an image of a man and woman walking hand in hand along the beach at sunset. Dreamy! Inside the card we both wrote our promise to the other. Our promise was to save ourselves *for* each other, even if it meant saving ourselves *from* each other until our honeymoon. We signed and dated the card and then placed it in the frame.

We hung the picture above the sofa in Ross's apartment. That was where we knew we would be most susceptible to slip up and go too far physically. That simple, signed agreement in our framed card became a steady reminder of the promise we had made to each other. The visual reminder helped to ensure that the gift of intimacy between us was guarded and preserved until our wedding day.

And, yes, it definitely was worth it. It still is all these years later.

> The secret things belong to the LORD our God, but the things revealed belong to us and to our children forever, that we may follow all the words of this law.
> —Deuteronomy 29:29 (NIV)

HOLD OUT

I will hold out for real love
I will hold out for intimacy
I will hold out until my heart is ready
I will hold out for God's timing
I will hold out for purity
I will hold out for just one man
I will hold out so that I can have butterflies
I will hold out for all that is sacred in God's eyes
I will hold out because I am a peculiar treasure
I will hold out when others around me are giving in
I will hold out as long as it takes
I will hold out my open heart to You, Lord
I will hold out my empty hand and wait
I will hold out for my future husband.
           —Rachel Gunn

Tricia:

The long-awaited day finally arrived. My wedding day. I stood at the doorway to the church wearing a white dress. A lot had happened in my past, but I trusted God had forgiven me. I stood there clean, forgiven, ready to start my new life with my soon-to-be husband. I had given my heart and life to Christ. He had pulled me out of the pit of pain and sin that I had found myself in. He had cleansed me by taking my sin on Him and giving me His purity instead. I knew that because of Christ,

God saw me standing in the church wearing the color of purity. White wasn't just a traditional color choice for me; it was a symbol of how I looked to God.

"Come now, let's settle this,"
     says the LORD.
"Though your sins are like scarlet,
     I will make them as white as snow.
Though they are red like crimson,
     I will make them as white as wool."
     —Isaiah 1:18 (NLT)

You know what? When I walked down the aisle and saw John's smile, he saw me that way too. Beautiful. Pure. His. In fact, even after being married twenty years, John still calls me his bride. "How's my bride today?" "Where would my bride like to go to dinner?" "What I'd love most right now is a kiss from my bride."

If you're like me and have acted in ways that made you impure, you don't have to hang on to those shameful feelings. God can cleanse you and make you pure. He wants that more than anything else.

And maybe, like me, you also worried that a good, godly guy would never want you. That such a man would see you as damaged goods. I'm testimony that it doesn't need to be the case. Start praying for that now—pray for your future husband to see you as the pure, beautiful woman Christ made you to be. A guy like that is out there. Trust. Believe.

When everything was hopeless, Abraham believed
anyway, deciding to live not on the basis of what
he saw he *couldn't* do but on what God said he
would do....

He didn't tiptoe around God's promise asking
cautiously skeptical questions. He plunged into the
promise and came up strong, ready for God, sure
that God would make good on what he had said....
But it's not just Abraham; it's also us!...we embrace
and believe the One who brought Jesus to life when
the conditions were equally hopeless. The sacrificed
Jesus made us fit for God, set us *right with God.*
—Romans 4:18–25 (MSG)

WHAT ABOUT YOU?

Robin:

What if God has the right man for you, ready and waiting in
the wings, but you're too emotionally engaged in the wrong
person to see beyond your immediate feelings? Break your
emotional engagement. Bind your heart to God's. Transfer
onto Christ all the emotional expressions of love you were pour-
ing into that guy.

Proverbs 31:10 (NASB) says, "An excellent wife, who can
find?" That seems to indicate the man is the one doing the
hunting and seeking. Come out of that jungle of emotional
tangles you have been hiding in with the wrong guy. Come out
into the light so you can be found.

Tricia:

Maybe you've already given away your heart. Maybe you've given more. Sometimes we only think we know what we're doing. Our hearts tell us what they want most of all, and we allow our minds and bodies to follow. Yet if you have to hide your choices, can they be good?

Even if you have given yourself away completely, you can choose to start again. You don't have to continue down that path. Today can be your new beginning. Just because you strayed away from God's perfect plan for you doesn't mean the rest of your life will be second-rate. The moment you surrender yourself to God, *from that moment,* you will have God's best. You are forgiven, pure.

Maybe you haven't given away your body, but what about your emotions? Have you thought, dreamed, hoped, and connected with someone and found yourself emotionally entangled? The untangling can begin today. You can start the healing that will prepare you for your future husband.

Take time right now to think about all the ways you've allowed your body, soul, and emotions to become tangled up in others' lives in unhealthy ways. Ask God to help you break those bonds. Even if the act felt right, think of it from Jesus' point of view. How did He feel about your giving yourself away completely to somebody who wasn't your husband? Take time to pray about that. Ask Jesus to forgive you for the ways you hurt Him by doing things outside of His perfectly designed will.

Also, during the upcoming days and weeks, spend time reading your Bible and praying. Ask Jesus to show you how He wants to be the Lover of your soul. Ask Him to help you feel that love in ways you have never felt it before. Thank Him for His forgiveness and restoration, and turn to Him whenever you feel yourself drawn to guys in unhealthy ways.

Of course, in all the ways you pray for yourself, pray for your future husband too.

How Do I Pray That My Future Husband Will Guard His Intimacy with Others?

- Pray that he will develop healthy emotional intimacy with the right people, such as those in his immediate family.
- Pray that he will guard his emotional, spiritual, and physical involvement with other women.
- Pray that he will develop close and healthy relationships with his friends.
- Pray that he will not give in to the temptation of being physically bonded to another person.
- Pray for his eyes, that he will look away from tempting images. Men are wired to follow after what their eyes see. Pray that he will guard his eyes.
- Pray for his mind, that he will focus on your future relationship rather than on temporary desires.

- Pray that, if your future husband has crossed
  boundaries, God will work in his heart and begin
  to heal him in his preparation for you.

Promise me, O women of Jerusalem,
   by the gazelles and wild deer,
   not to awaken love until the time is right.
   —Song of Songs 3:5 (NLT)

SHE PRAYED…GOD ANSWERED

I prayed for my husband from the time I was in junior high. I prayed for his purity and that he would grow strong in the Lord. I married when I was twenty-three after praying for him for about ten years. My parents prayed for him too.

One of my most treasured memories was when my dad walked me down the aisle at my wedding, and he whispered to me, "There's our answered prayer."

My husband has definitely been just that. —Becky

A PRAYER FOR MY FUTURE HUSBAND

Dear Lord, I pray for my future husband today. I pray for his purity. That he will turn to You to keep him pure. Or, if he's already made other choices, that he would turn to You to make him white as snow.

Lord, I know it's easy to entangle our emotions with others, just like it's easy to entangle our bodies. I pray that my future husband will guard his body, soul, and spirit until the time You have designed for us to commit our whole lives to each other.

And I pray that, when we do meet, You will help us to be pure in our relationship. I pray we won't stumble as we near the end of the race toward each other. Thank You, God, for designing purity in this way. It's a gift. It's freedom. Help my future husband to see it as such. Amen.

A Prayer for Me

Lord, I know I'm designed to be intimate with another. I know this because my feelings stir inside when I see romantic movies or read romantic books. I pray that I will not awaken this desire until the time is right. Teach me how to bond emotionally with You. Help me make good choices that will protect not only my body, soul, and spirit but also my desires.

For all the ways I've bonded to another, physically and emotionally and even in the wrong way spiritually, I pray You will break those bonds. Forgive me, Jesus, for the ways I've turned to other people while You have been waiting for me to turn to You.

Help me, Lord, to understand good intimacy—with my family and my friends. I know that having good relationships with others whom You bring into my life will help me to know how to be in a good relationship with my future husband.

Finally, Lord, help me to understand You are the Son of Man. You understand what it is like to love, to cry, to embrace. Fill me with Your love. I ask this in Jesus' name, amen.

When I look at Jesus' warm and intimate friendships,
my heart fills with praise that Jesus was…a man. A man
of flesh-and-blood reality. His heart felt the sting of
sympathy. His eyes glowed with tenderness. His arms
embraced. His lips smiled. His hands touched. Jesus was
male! Jesus invites us to relate to him as the Son of Man.
And because he is fully man, we can relate to Jesus with
affection and love.

—Joni Eareckson Tada

My Thoughts ON MY FUTURE HUSBAND AND ME BEING GOOD LOVERS

DISCUSSION QUESTIONS

1. What does it mean to you that you can call Jesus
   friend?

11

Pray

for "The List"

Don't judge by his appearance or height,
for I have rejected him.
The LORD doesn't see things the way you see them.
People judge by outward appearance,
but the LORD looks at the heart.

—1 SAMUEL 16:7 (NLT)

Robin:

So, go ahead. Be honest. Tell us: Do you have a list?

You know what list we're talking about here—the wish list that specifies all your personal preferences for Mr. Amazing-and-Wonderful. Some women have the particulars down to height, weight, and eye color. Other women have a short list that reads like a want ad with only the basics listed: "Must be a Christian and love me." They figure that's a great starting point, and they'll let God decide the details.

One woman told me she kept adding to her list and now has nine pages of specifics, including which musical instrument he needs to play and in which month he needs to have been born. Seriously.

If you're going to keep a list, be fair about it. And realistic. What if your future husband was composing nine pages of requirements for you right now? You can't exactly change your birth date.

One friend sent me a note after a painful breakup with a guy she really liked. She poked fun at the list she had written during high school and said now that she was older and more experienced in the challenges of relationships, she had narrowed down her list:

Still breathing
Not too big of a jerk
Speaks English
Number 3 is optional

How about if we look at the list God gave that helps us to identify true love:

Love is patient and kind. Love is not jealous or boastful or proud or rude. It does not demand its own way. It is not irritable, and it keeps no record of being wronged. It does not rejoice about injustice but rejoices whenever the truth wins out. Love never gives up, never loses faith, is

always hopeful, and endures through every
circumstance.

—1 Corinthians 13:4–7 (NLT)

When I was in my twenties, I found a poem written by
a woman when she was about my same age. Her lyrical list
changed my opinion of the sorts of specifics I should value
as I created my own list and presented it to the Lord as a
heartfelt request. This young woman asked God for several
highly specific character qualities, and—wow!—did God
ever answer her with equally specific qualities in the man
she married.

Here's the poem. I think you'll see what I mean.

Dear God

Dear God, I prayed, all unafraid
(as we're inclined to do)
I do not need a handsome man
But let him be like You;
I do not need one big and strong
Nor yet so very tall,
Nor need he be some genius
Or wealthy, Lord, at all;
But let his head be high, dear God,
And let his eye be clear,
His shoulders straight, whate'er his state,
Whate'er his earthly sphere;

And let his face have character,
A ruggedness of soul,
And let his whole life show, dear God,
A singleness of goal;
Then when he comes (as he will come)
With quiet eyes aglow,
I'll understand that he's the man
I prayed for long ago.[1]

Are you curious to know who wrote this poem? Her name was Ruth Bell. She wrote this poetic list in 1939 when she was nineteen years old. On August 13, 1943, Ruth married God's answer to this prayer—his name was Billy Graham. This famous God Lover and evangelist spent his life living out that "ruggedness of soul." He definitely had a face with character as well as "quiet eyes aglow." And talk about a life with a "singleness of goal"! Ruth listed these specifics before she even met Billy.

When I read Ruth's poem, what I observed and took seriously was that she focused on the inward character qualities of the man she was asking God to bring into her life. We don't just marry the outward appearance of a man. As my sister told me years ago, we marry the heart.

When you link the deepest, most vulnerable part of yourself with your husband, you are, in essence, marrying his truest self. It's only a matter of time before that truest self comes out in both partners. When you get sick and are dependent on your

---

[1] *Sitting by My Laughing Fire*, by Ruth Bell Graham, © 1977 The Ruth Graham Literary Trust, used by permission, all rights reserved.

spouse to care for you, it will matter a whole lot more that he is a man of compassion than that he has great abs.

> Give ear, our God, and hear.... We do not make
> requests of you because we are righteous, but because of
> your great mercy.
> —Daniel 9:18 (NIV)

Tricia:

I don't think I ever wrote down a list when I first became interested in guys. Maybe it would have helped if I had. As I reflect on the guys I dated in high school, I liked tall guys with blue eyes. These guys were athletic, and they seemed to have no problems getting girlfriends. I thought "fighting for your man" was part of the process. Now I see it brought a lot of drama, with a side of heartbreak and insecurities.

If I had a list of anything, it was of my personal characteristics that made me feel "not good enough." I always felt large compared to my size 0 friends, my teeth were crooked, my clothes weren't stylish enough, and I was more quiet than bold. That list wasn't written down either, but I carried it around. In my mind. In my heart.

Later, even after I gave my heart to Jesus, I worried. First, because I was pregnant. (A huge turnoff to potential boyfriends, right?) After that, I was worried because of the baby fat and stretch marks. As a new Christian, I still struggled with my temper and my attitude, and I didn't know much about the Bible. Again, the list of ways I didn't measure up scrolled through my mind every time I looked in the mirror or said something stupid.

When I met John, I realized he was different from the guys I had dated before. He was tall, but he wasn't athletic. He had brown eyes, and he didn't walk around with pride and arrogance as though he was better than everyone else. I liked that. Mostly, I loved his heart. Patient, kind, forgiving, truthful, not self-seeking. He was everything I needed in a husband—things I hadn't thought to look for.

As the years have passed, I have grown to appreciate other qualities John possesses:

- He loves children.
- He has a great love for the Word of God.
- He is a hard worker.
- He is a great leader.
- He is a man of his word.

And my list? I'm still not the size I want to be. I still wish I had a better wardrobe and a bolder personality, but those things don't seem to matter as much anymore. It's amazing how your self-esteem increases when you see love reflected in another person's gaze.

Pray That Your Future Husband Will Marry You for What He Sees in Your Heart

I've also grown closer to God over the years, and I've come to a greater understanding that God designed who I am for a purpose. Since God makes no mistakes, I'm not a mistake.

Now this is The List I cling to, and it comes from God's heart:

1. "I have loved you with an everlasting love; I have drawn you with unfailing kindness" (Jeremiah 31:3, NIV).

2. "Do not fear, for I have redeemed you; I have summoned you by name; you are mine" (Isaiah 43:1, NIV).

3. "When you pass through the waters, I will be with you; and when you pass through the rivers, they will not sweep over you. When you walk through the fire, you will not be burned; the flames will not set you ablaze" (Isaiah 43:2, NIV).

Finally, after so many years of not caring about God's Word, I have dug into it and now understand how much God adores me. In fact, Zephaniah 3:17 is my favorite verse:

The LORD your God is with you,
   the Mighty Warrior who saves.
He will take great delight in you;
   in his love he will no longer rebuke you,
   but will rejoice over you with singing. (NIV)

If God's list is like that, how can I be hard on myself? Realizing how intensely God loves me helps me understand even more how much of a gift John is to me. Though John is not perfect, God knew he was what I needed. He knew John would complete me and work beside me in the labor God created us to do together.

The List, you see, isn't just about what things will make you happy, or who would look good at your side. God's list, as He formed your future husband, was to create the other half of you so together you make a whole unit. He created someone with you in mind.

Have you ever heard the saying "Opposites attract"? That's only part of it. Two different people with unique parts not only attract, but they also complete.

Don't be afraid to write a list; just be open to changing it over time. Your idea of Mr. Amazing-and-Wonderful *will* change…as God changes and transforms you.

What About You?

Do you have a list? Does your list focus more on the physical characteristics of what you would like in a future husband, or does it focus on his character qualities?

If your future husband made a list today of the qualities he would like in his future wife, which ones would match qualities already present in your life?

On the following page is a list of character qualities. Go through and circle the top ten you would appreciate in a future mate. After you are done, look at the list again. Which ones would you like to pray for God to help *you* with? Put a star by those.

And remember, no nine-page lists! All of these character qualities are admirable, but which are most important to you?

- A good listener
- A people person
- Attentive
- Bold
- Cautious, doesn't make rash decisions
- Compassionate, generous
- Conforms to God, not to the world
- Content
- Creative
- Decisive
- Dependable
- Determined
- Diligent
- Discerning
- Does right things, modeling Christ
- Encouraging
- Enjoys family
- Enthusiastic
- Faithful
- Flexible
- Forgiving
- Gentle
- Has a sense of humor
- Has endurance
- Heavenly focused
- Humble
- Joyful and thankful
- Loving
- Loyal
- Obedient
- Orderly
- Patient
- Punctual
- Pure
- Resourceful
- Responsible
- Reverent
- Secure
- Seeks God's wisdom
- Seeks justice
- Self-controlled
- Sensitive
- Sincere
- Thorough
- Thoughtful
- Thrifty
- Trusts God's timing
- Truthful
- Wise
- Works for the Lord, not for man

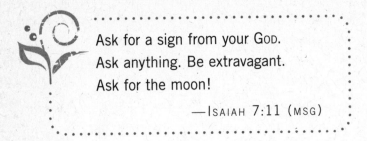

> Ask for a sign from your GOD.
> Ask anything. Be extravagant.
> Ask for the moon!
>
> —ISAIAH 7:11 (MSG)

HOW DO I PRAY FOR STRONG CHARACTER QUALITIES IN MY FUTURE HUSBAND?

- Pray he will be inwardly motivated to do what is right.
- Pray he will seek God with his whole heart.
- Pray he will respond with trust and faith in God in all situations.
- Pray he will be wise in handling difficult situations.
- Pray he will do what is right, even when no one is looking.

SHE PRAYED...GOD ANSWERED

I actually made a list of all the things I wanted in a husband...Christian, sense of humor, kind, etc. (it was really long and got pretty specific on little things). I prayed all through college that whoever it was would stay strong in his faith and not do anything he would

God also wants men to be free to demonstrate tenderness, sensitivity, understanding, meekness, and humility. Free to be vulnerable enough to foster intimacy and to shed tears.

The freedom of authentic masculinity...produces a "divine elasticity" in men. Finally they can lead with firmness, then submit with humility. They can challenge with a cutting edge, then encourage with enthusiasm. They can fight aggressively for just causes, then moments later weep over suffering....

Secure, free, authentic men leave a mark—on their colleagues, friends, wives, and especially their children.

—Bill Hybels, *Honest to God?*

My Thoughts ON MY FUTURE HUSBAND AND ME DEVELOPING STRONG CHARACTER QUALITIES

DISCUSSION QUESTIONS

1. Is the list of qualities you want in your future husband written down or in your head? What are some of the items on it?

2. In what ways might we not be fair when making our lists?

3. What stands out to you in God's list in 1 Corinthians 13?

4. What line in Ruth Bell Graham's poem do you like best? Why?

5. Do you have a list of who you should be? Is such a list helpful or hurtful? Explain.

6. Do you have a hard time believing God takes great delight in you? Why or why not?

7. Do you agree with the statement "Opposites attract"? Why or why not?

8. Often we surround ourselves with people who are like us. In what ways might God use your future husband's differences to complete you?

9. Are you ready to make a list of ways you can change to prepare for your future husband?

12

Pray

for Contentment

But godliness with contentment
is great gain.

—1 TIMOTHY 6:6 (NIV)

Robin:

Fifteen years ago on a breezy September afternoon I stood as a
beaming bridesmaid in a lovely Southern California rose garden. The beautiful bride stepped forward and met her groom
under a white lattice arch where they held hands and made
promises before God and an intimate gathering of family and
friends. My dear friend had waited well into her forties to experience this exquisite moment. Now that her long-prayed-for day
had come, this man clearly had been worth the wait.

How had Katherine spent those decades of singleness? She
lived. Katherine didn't wait around for a husband to show up
before she bought a home or traveled to interesting places she always had wanted to see. She didn't collapse her life; she expanded

it. One of the areas where she decided to expand was by becoming more active in a singles group at church. Katherine helped to form the group and plan get-togethers and outings. The group began to grow as more single adults found out that her church was the place to be.

When she called and told me about a certain interesting and handsome man she had met in the singles group, I could just picture how irresistible she must have been to him. The life she had crafted for herself was full and beautiful and brimming with contentment. She was quite different from several other women who frequented the group with sour spirits and expressions that broadcast, "Go ahead. I dare you to be nice to me." They were the ones who could be overheard saying, "There just aren't any good men left out there for women like us."

Contentment shows. It's the best face-lift, spirit-brightener, heart-toner remedy out there.

> I've kept my feet on the ground,
>   I've cultivated a quiet heart.
> Like a baby content in its mother's arms,
>   my soul is a baby content.
> —Psalm 131:2 (MSG)

Contentment is a treasure in marriage too. Five months into our marriage, Ross lost something very dear to him. His TR6 convertible sports car was stolen in the middle of the night from the open parking stall at our apartment. He had bought the vintage beauty a few months before we started to date seriously, and he spent hours replacing parts and tuning the engine until the little honey purred just right. The first gift he ever bought me was a hat so that, when we went out cruising around with the top down, my long hair wouldn't get blown into tangles.

We both loved that car. Our favorite cheap date as starving newlyweds was to jump in the TR6 just before sunset and rumble our way down the Pacific Coast Highway.

The police officer who filled out the report on the stolen car told us a rare vehicle like Ross's was worth four to ten times its value in parts. The chances of our ever seeing the little brown TR6 again were nil.

Once the shock wore off and we found out what we could expect to see in the insurance check, I asked Ross if he wanted to try to find another TR6 to fix up. I knew how much happiness that car had brought him.

"No, we need a more reliable car." He reminded me that the old VW I had bought from my brother-in-law for four hundred dollars was wheezing and gasping every time I tried to coax her over forty miles per hour.

"But you loved that little TR6. Fixing it up was your hobby. I hate to think of your not having another car like that. It was a big part of your life."

Then Ross said something that endeared him to me even more, if that were possible. "I have you, and I have Jesus. I am content."

Over the years I've thought of how different our married life would have been if he hadn't been content to say good-bye to the TR6. We could have easily spent thousands of dollars replacing the car, keeping it running, storing it safely, and insuring it. The automobile was a luxury item, and no item should ever be so essential in our lives that we can't be happy unless we have it.

In a deeper, unspoken way, when Ross told me he was content, I felt secure as a wife. I believed my husband was content to have me as his wife, and he wasn't going to keep a lookout on the sly for someone else. He was content with what God had given him.

Pray That Your Future Husband Will Be Content

Every marriage goes through seasons of loss and gain. Every couple needs to make difficult decisions on how and where their limited finances will be directed. Contentment in all situations allows room for flexibility. Contentment opens up new options. Contentment brings peace.

> I have learned how to be content with whatever I have. I
> know how to live on almost nothing or with everything.
> I have learned the secret of living in every situation,
> whether it is with a full stomach or empty, with plenty
> or little. For I can do everything through Christ, who
> gives me strength.
> —Philippians 4:11–13 (NLT)

Tricia:

Recently John and I made a cross-country move. John was excited about starting his job for a new ministry. I was excited for him, but I was also sad about leaving old friends. In the wonderful way God works, He brought me a new friend and neighbor, Michelle.

In the short months I've known her, Michelle has gone on a research trip with me and has become my accountability partner and workout buddy. Even more than that, she listens and cares.

Michelle is in her thirties and is beautiful and single. I'm not sure why some guy didn't snatch her up long ago. Although Michelle's desire is to be married and have a family, she doesn't sit around and lament the fact that it hasn't happened yet. Michelle mentors a group of teen girls and works with teen moms. She works in radio and helps disseminate Christian broadcasts around the world. She plays pranks on friends, goes on twenty-five-mile bike rides, and travels the country.

Michelle's not on the Internet looking at singles' Web sites every night. She's willing to try a blind date but doesn't prowl the town for men.

When I asked her about this, Michelle had this to say:

I'm a thirty-something single and have always jokingly blamed my singleness on my mother because she didn't pray for my future husband. Then awhile back I was convicted when a friend told me that I should be praying for him. I started to pray that my future husband would be full of love for God, that God would be his delight. I asked God to equip him with strength and wisdom to be a man who leads. On and on I prayed, thinking that, *bam,* soon God would deliver my heart's desire.

See, I didn't want to be alone any longer; I wanted someone to hold me, someone to laugh with, someone to dream with, someone to tell me I looked beautiful even with the awful new haircut, someone to do life with, someone to balance the checkbook. But really what happened is that God smoothed over the deep, deep desire and helped me to deal with my longings and not be so consumed with what I didn't have.

Last year I was going through a longer-than-normal valley of these intense feelings of wanting to be married, and I finally asked God to romance my soul. I prayed that He would be the one I laughed with, the one who made me feel treasured, the one I shared my deepest thoughts with, the one to fill my mind every waking hour, the one I would serve self-sacrificially for the rest of my life.

What a ride God took me on. No, my intense longing for a husband didn't go away instantly. It took some time for God to fill every empty cavity of my life, but He did. I learned that it wasn't about me and my timing and my wants or desires (even if they were good). My life, single or married, is about Him and how I reflect Him each day.

Don't get me wrong, I still struggle with wanting what many of my friends have—the white-picket fence, two-car garage, a couple of car seats in the back of a midsize SUV ('cause I'm determined not to buy a minivan). Many of them tell me that when they finally surrendered their lives to Him, God dropped a man on their doorstep. But don't buy into that lie. There is no special formula to follow. It's not pray this much, surrender this much, and you get the guy. Nope. God doesn't work that way. He answers prayer with what's going to glorify Him the most. My single life may be bringing Him more honor than my life with a husband and three kids.

I do want to be married someday…but till then I am free to serve Him in numerous ways, spend as much time as I want with Him, pray for my future husband, and—bonus—I am in total control of my TV remote.

What About You?

Are you finding ways to live your life to the fullest rather than waiting for a husband to come along before your adventures really begin? When you go through rough times—when jobs and people you love are taken from you—are you learning to say, as the apostle Paul did, that you can be content in every situation (see Philippians 4:12)? Are you willing to wait? If you *know* that God's best for you means waiting until you're twenty-five, thirty, forty…or never, are you willing to trust Him? Are you willing to live the life He calls you to? Are you willing to let Him be the Lover of your soul?

WHAT IS THE POINT?

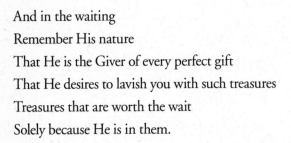

The point in waiting is
to enjoy
To love and worship God
In every act of your life

Including the waiting.

And in the waiting
Remember His nature
That He is the Giver of every perfect gift
That He desires to lavish you with such treasures
Treasures that are worth the wait
Solely because He is in them.

Rest in this:
He is going to give you
Exactly what you need
At exactly the time you need it.
That is reason to smile

That is reason to breathe easy
And rest in Him.

Let go of "when" and "if"
Because His ways
Are so much higher than yours.
His thoughts
Beyond what you could ever fathom
Because He loves you.
Oh, how He loves you.
And that is the point
of your entire existence
To experience His presence
His love
Inside every moment

Especially in the waiting.
　　—Josiah Schwartz

SHE PRAYED...GOD ANSWERED

Being single is tough. Especially when you hear over and over again that, when you're ready, when you're spiritual enough or thin enough or emotionally together enough, God will bring your husband along. All of which means, you're not "enough." For me, decades passed, and I had prayed every prayer about marriage that I could imagine.

Still, no husband put in an appearance. My sense of how flawed I must be became ingrained. I often flailed around in prayer about how I didn't seem to be able to pass some test I wasn't even aware I was taking.

Eventually God pointed out to me that He wasn't measuring "enoughness." Marriage wasn't like earning a Girl Scout badge, with the lessons learned ticked off until you had enough points. Instead, marriage was a gift that He chose to bestow on some, not to bestow on others—His choice, as is true of all good gifts.

Once I realized I couldn't earn a husband—through prayer, through passing tests, through any method known to man—I set out to follow what I had been called to: live richly and contentedly the life God had given to me. I decided to quit circling my jet plane around the airport of marriage and take off sans a spouse. I soared into a romance with God that grows deeper and richer with each day. My prayers turned from fussing over where my very tardy husband could be to savoring my relationship with God. And, oh yes, God did bestow the gift of marriage on me many years after I chose to soar, and I happily welcomed my beloved into my full life. —Katherine

> Give Him time to do great things. The greater the work
> He plans, the greater the prayer preparation that may be
> necessary, including prayer for guidance. God often
> waits so that He can be even more gracious.
> —Wesley L. Duewel

A Prayer for My Future Husband

Dear Lord, I pray for the man You have planned for me, and I will continue to pray even if it takes years and years until I meet him. I pray, Lord, that if Your plan for us to be together is later rather than sooner, You will give him patience. I pray that His heart will not be hardened against You because of the waiting. I pray that he will not try to fill the hole with unhealthy habits or ungodly things. I pray he will turn to You, and You will fill him with love.

I also pray that my future husband will be content with whatever You give him and whatever You take away. No one in life gets everything he wants, and I pray my future husband will strive for heavenly things rather than earthly desires. In Jesus' name, amen.

A Prayer for Me

Dear Lord, I have to admit that I would like to imagine meeting my future husband sooner rather than later. I have to admit I'm not very good at waiting, and I tend to get impatient. Yet I know, Lord, that Your plan is perfect. I know You love me completely. If Your perfect plan means waiting, then I accept that. When I'm not happy about the waiting, I'll turn to You to help me be content. Jesus, I'm thankful that You'll be with me as I wait.

In a world that is shouting at me to want more, more, now, now, I pray You will help me be content. Speak to my mind and my heart when I want things I can't have or when my longings have me looking more to wants than needs. I know, Lord, You won't give

*me everything I want, but I'm thankful that You give me everything
I need.*

*Lord, I ask You to be the guide of my life. I want to live my life
to the fullest. I desire to be on the adventure with You. If You
choose for my future husband to join me right away on that adventure, thank You. If You choose to wait, thank You. I trust You,
Jesus. Amen.*

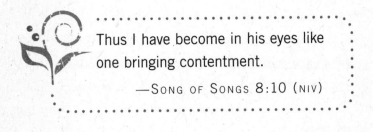

Thus I have become in his eyes like
one bringing contentment.

—Song of Songs 8:10 (niv)

My Thoughts ON MY FUTURE HUSBAND
AND ME BEING CONTENT

DISCUSSION QUESTIONS

1. What dreams will you pursue while waiting for your future husband?

2. What are some of the things you cherish most? If they were taken away, how would you feel?

3. Why do you think it's important to pray that your future husband will be content?

4. Why is it important to pray the same for yourself?

5. Read Philippians 4:11–13. In what ways have you learned to be content?

6. How can you grow your relationship with God—your true love—while you wait for your future husband?

7. Are you willing to live the life God calls you to—even
    if it doesn't include marriage? How can you make God
    the Lover of your soul?

8. What defines you?
    ____ God
    ____ Your belongings
    ____ Your personality
    ____ Your past mistakes
    ____ Your personal achievements
    ____ All of the above

9. Based on your answer, do you need to make adjust-
    ments to your sense of yourself?

10. What stood out most to you in Josiah Schwartz's
    poem? Why?

11. Do you think of marriage as a gift or as a reward
    for work you've done? Do your actions match your
    answer? If so, how? Do you need to make adjustments
    to your thoughts? to your actions?

13

Pray

for Commitment

Commit to the LORD whatever you do,
and he will establish your plans.

—PROVERBS 16:3 (NIV)

Robin:

When our son was fifteen, he went to summer camp. On the
last day a girl invited him to meet her that night down by the
water. She told him she had decided he was going to be the first
guy she ever kissed, and he could kiss her that night. Not much
seems to have changed about summer camp since I was a girl!

One thing did change, though. A new generation of young
men was told that true love waits, and they believed it. Our son
(also named Ross like his dad) is one of those young men. He
decided not to go down to the water that night to meet the
ready-to-be-kissed girl. Instead, he made a different decision.
He decided to make a purity ring for himself out of duct tape.
Yes, duct tape.

The girl had approached Ross when he was helping to disassemble one of the meeting tents at the camp. As she walked away, he spur-of-the-moment pulled on a long piece of duct tape that had been holding up the center pole. It struck him that the single piece of tape was an example of strength, displaying so much power and affecting the well-being of so many people.

Ross twisted the long strip into a loose-fitting ring that he circled around his ankle. He added more twisted layers until he had a crazy-looking manacle that could only be removed by cutting it off. People at camp asked him if he had lost the leash to his Boogie Board, because it looked like the ankle strap was still on his foot.

He returned home from camp with the unique adornment, and of course, I asked what it was.

"Something to help me remember my promise."

"What sort of promise?"

"To save my kisses and everything else for my future wife. When I get married, I'll give her a pair of scissors, and she'll be the one to cut this off my ankle."

Ross made that commitment when he was fifteen. By eighteen, he still was wearing the band and adding another layer to where the original ring was wearing thin. When he was twenty-one and living on his own more than four thousand miles away from home, he still kept his promise. At twenty-five, the ankle promise bracelet was still firmly in place and so was his commitment to his future wife, even though he had not yet met her.

The band was impossible to hide. Even under his socks one

could see he had something thick around his ankle. He was teased about being under house arrest. He received strange stares when new friends would ask what it was.

Over the years Ross kept up a tradition of adding a reinforcing layer of duct tape as the current layer wore thin. As he shored up the thickening ankle bracelet, he asked God to remember him and to bring into his life a godly woman who also was saving herself for him. The older he got, the number of women who were continuing to "hold out for a hero" was becoming more and more sparse.

But there was one. And yes, she was The One. The one woman God had been preparing for our son since before he was born.

A few weeks after our son's twenty-seventh birthday, he stood at the altar with a smile on his face that made his mama's heart soar. His beloved bride, adorned in shimmering white, came walking down the aisle toward him. This was the day for which both of them had waited. Nothing in their past detracted from the sacredness of this moment.

When my son kissed his bride, the guests broke into applause. Then the bride and groom joined hands, made their exit down the aisle, and drew apart from all the guests who were more than ready to celebrate. Ross handed his new wife a pair of scissors. She cut and cut at all the layers of duct tape until the promise band came off his ankle.

A promise kept for twelve years.

Kisses that rightfully belonged to his bride were not frivolously spent on a girl at summer camp. Instead, Ross made a decision the summer he was fifteen. He chose to start his commitment to his future wife long before he met her. All those kisses that could have been spent on lots of other willing girls during those twelve years of waiting had been saved and stored.

My son gave his wife two wedding gifts that day. The first was a pair of diamond earrings, and the second was his promise kept. I don't think I need to tell you which one had the greater value in the eyes and heart of his bride.

Pray That Your Future Husband Will Make Lasting Commitments

Faith makes us sure of what we hope for and gives us proof of what we cannot see.
—Hebrews 11:1 (CEV)

Tricia:

I remember snuggling with my two-year-old son, Cory, and praying for his future wife. It seemed strange in a way. I mean, we were dealing with potty training and learning to count to ten!

As Cory grew older, his loving nature shone. Cory is the one who would give me a hug in front of his friends. When he grew taller than me, he would greet me with a kiss on the forehead every morning. I knew his wife would be a lucky lady someday. His tender and caring heart would be a wonderful gift to his future bride.

Cory had a few girlfriends in high school, and with each of them he made his goal known. He was saving himself, his purity, for his future wife. That made me happy. Cory was born to a teen mom out of wedlock, but that didn't affect how he was going to live his life for God. If anything, it strengthened his resolve. He had seen my pain. He had heard me talk about my heartache, and he was choosing a better way.

As Cory grew older, I continued to pray for his future wife. I knew he was praying for her too. Sometimes I would look at a girl who was his friend and think, *Is she The One?* At times it seemed I was nearly as eager as he was to finally meet the young woman I had been praying for so long.

Cory came home from work one afternoon and told me about a young woman named Katie whom he had met at volleyball. His face brightened as he talked about her fun personality, her positive outlook on life, her love of God, and how adorable she was. When John and I met Katie, we fell in love with her too. I prayed more. Cory and Katie did too. They both had been waiting and hoping. They both had saved all of themselves. Now they wondered if their prayers were soon to be answered.

Last summer I sat in the front row at my son's wedding. Tears came to my eyes seeing the bride *and the groom* in white. Cory had waited—saved himself for his bride. She had waited— saved herself for him. They entered into their marriage free from past bonds.

When I saw Katie put the ring on Cory's hand, my heart leaped. He was committing to this young woman for life. I knew the road ahead of them wouldn't be perfect, but I also knew their commitment in the little things—family, friends, faith, service to name a few—had prepared them for this larger, holier commitment.

There she is, I thought, looking at my new daughter-in-law. *The girl of my prayers. The woman of my son's dreams.*

I have three more kids I'm still praying for, and I'm excited to see what God has in store for them. I know that diligent prayers are always answered, but it's up to each of us to make the commitment. It's up to us to stand strong while others fall. I know my son is thankful that he did. I know Katie is too.

> Kiss me and kiss me again,
>> for your love is sweeter than wine.
>> —Song of Songs 1:2 (NLT)

What About You?

Are you frivolously spending your kisses, or are you saving them for The One to whom they rightfully belong? Are you a person who can be depended on to keep her promise? If you say you'll do something or be somewhere at a certain time, can your friends and family depend on you to keep your word? Do you see yourself as the answer to someone's (many people's) prayers?

> When you make a promise to God, don't delay in
> following through, for God takes no pleasure in fools.
> Keep all the promises you make to him.
>> —Ecclesiastes 5:4 (NLT)

SHE PRAYED...GOD ANSWERED

Ever since I was little, I was told that whoever I ended up marrying was going to be someone very special. So whenever I looked at a guy as a possible boyfriend, I knew he had to be something special or he wasn't the right one for me. I remember listening to a song in which the girl is praying that her future husband will wait for her and save himself for her. I had never heard of that before...praying for the man you're going to marry when you haven't even met him yet. How cool! I started to pray for my future husband then. I prayed that he would wait for me and knew I wanted to wait for him.

Just about seven years later, I met Cory. I didn't know that he was going to be the man that I would marry. I did know he was a God Lover, and I began to pray for him to stay strong in his beliefs and to hold fast to what we had both been saving for our future spouses. I also prayed that he would become the man of my dreams. Little did I know that it wouldn't take me very long to notice that Cory indeed WAS the man of my dreams. Praying for my future husband helped me to figure out exactly what I wanted, needed, and couldn't live without in a husband. God answered my prayers more than I ever imagined. —Katie

How Can I Pray for My Future Husband to Keep His Commitments?

- Pray that he will be faithful in the small things, such as following through on what he promises to do.
- Pray that he will see you as the rightful receiver of all his expressions of intimate physical affection and place all his kisses into a "piggy bank," saving them for you.
- Pray that others in his life will join him in praying for his future wife—for you.
- Pray for his faith to grow—that he'll continue to live right and wait, even when he can't see you coming.

True faith manifests itself through our actions.

—Francis Chan

A Prayer for My Future Husband

Dear Heavenly Father, many guys are out there who shy away from being committed, from doing the right thing, but I pray my future husband won't be one of them. Lord, I pray that You will give him a resolve to save himself—all of himself—for me. I pray that You will give him the strength to follow through. I pray You will give him patience and endurance as the years pass.

Lord, I'm thankful that heroes still exist, and I'm looking forward to meeting mine. May his faith fuel his actions in all things big and small. May he learn to be committed in all aspects of life in preparation for the commitment of our marriage.

I pray that You won't leave him alone in his journey, but that You will bring others around to pray with him and for him. I know that with his prayers, my prayers, and the prayers of others, Your perfect plan will come to pass here on earth.

Thank You for the commitment You have made to my future husband, Lord, to always be there for him. I praise You for that. In Your name, amen.

A Prayer for Me

Lord God, I picked up this book excited about saying all the right prayers so You would bring me my future husband. What I didn't expect was to be challenged in so many areas. Lord, I know today I need to change. I need to be committed.

For so many years, Lord, I thought about what I wanted without thinking about what I could give. I know now that what I give is an amazing gift. First, my prayers, then my heart, then my commitment.

Father, I know that I won't be perfect until heaven, but I don't want to use that as an excuse not to seek You and ask You to transform me. Show me all the areas where I don't follow through as I should. Make me strong to live as I should. May my commitment to my future husband grow each day. In Your name, amen.

Let us hold unswervingly to the hope we profess, for he who promised is faithful.
—Hebrews 10:23 (NIV)

This is the secret of joy. We shall no longer strive for our own way; but commit ourselves, easily and simply, to God's way, acquiesce in His will, and in so doing find our peace.
—Evelyn Underhill

DISCUSSION QUESTIONS

1. How is your life displaying that you're willing to hold out for a hero?

2. In what areas of your life do you need greater faith?

3. What couples in your life are faithful and committed in their journey with each other? Who are they, and how do they inspire you?

4. Are you frivolously spending your kisses, or are you saving them for the one to whom they rightfully belong? What can you do to remind yourself to remain committed to your future husband (such as using duct tape, as Ross did, or wearing a ring or necklace symbolizing purity)?

5. What have you done to cause your friends and family to describe you as dependable?

6. What have you done to deserve the descriptor "undependable"?

7. What changes do you want to make to other people's opinions of you? How can you convince them you've changed?

8. What does the word *commitment* mean to you?

9. Faith is shown best by our actions. How have your actions proven your faith lately?

10. How have your actions proven your commitment to your future husband?

11. Who in your life is joining you in praying for your future husband? How do their prayers help?

12. Who else can you ask to pray with you concerning your future husband?

A *Closing Thought*

from Robin and Tricia

We all adore a beautiful love story. We gravitate toward just such stories in our selection of movies, novels, and music. We feel the journey right along with the actors, or the characters, or in the lyrics. Despite the obstacles, heartaches, and challenges, when we observe a declaration of love, a commitment, and a coming together of two people in a romance, it resonates deep in our spirit and makes us just want to let out a great big sigh. We all want our own version to be part of our life stories.

The mystery of it all is that you don't know if your life story will have a grand love story in it. But you *do* know that you're part of a greater, eternal romance. A very real Bridegroom has promised to one day come riding in on a white horse and to take you away to be with Him forever.

Thinking back to Elizabeth's soul-stirring story and the words from her letters to her future husband reminds us that the ultimate love story is the story of God's unfailing love for us. He calls us "the Bride of Christ" and invites us to the wedding feast of the Lamb. All the longings embedded in our hearts to be sought, found, desired, and loved forever are placed there by the One who created us. Remember, God is the Relentless Lover. We are His First Love, and He has never stopped pursuing us because He wants us to be with Him forever. Every earthly love story borrows its theme from this eternal story written by the Author and Finisher of our faith (see Hebrews 12:2, KJV).

Will your earthly love story come true? For many of you, it will. The coming together of your future husband and you could be in the near future…or it could be years in the distance. It could be a quick romance. It could be a slow falling in love. It could be exactly like you pictured it or like nothing you ever dreamed. For every woman who has trusted her life to Christ, our greatest love story will be fully realized, as it was for Elizabeth, when we enter heaven and lift our eyes to look into the face of our Beloved for the first time.

When the day comes that your love story is celebrated by your closest friends and family, you'll know that every prayer was worth it. Every whispered word from a tender heart is precious to God. No request is ignored. No moment spent with your Heavenly Father is wasted.

You might even wish you had prayed more. Why? Because your prayers are the first gifts you will give to your future husband. Gifts in which heaven participates. Gifts sent ahead before the two of you have even met. How cool is that?

We have one other secret we wanted to share with you. As we were writing this book, we have been praying for you. Yes, even though we don't know who will find this book and read it, we are praying now for all who read these words and let these verses sink into their hearts. We are asking God to raise up a powerful tribe of God-Lover Girls who will do battle now in the spiritual realm for the men of this generation. You are invited to become one of these quiet warriors. You have work to do. You already have everything you need to join in, and you know what to do. As we said at the beginning of this book, prayer is an extraordinary mystery. What exactly will happen once you start praying for your future husband?

There's only one way to find out...

PRAY!

God's timing is not ours to command.
If we do not start the fire with the first strike
of our match, we must try again.
God does hear our prayer,
but He may not answer it at the precise time
we have appointed in our own minds.
Instead, He will reveal Himself to our seeking hearts,
though not necessarily when and where we may expect.
Therefore we have a need for perseverance
and steadfast determination in our life of prayer....
May we, therefore, never despair.
God's time for mercy will come—
in fact, it has already come,
if our time for believing has arrived.
Ask in faith without wavering,
but never cease to petition the King
simply because He has delayed His reply.
Strike the match again and make the sparks fly.
Yet be sure to have your tinder ready,
for you will get a fire before long.

—CHARLES SPURGEON,
STREAMS IN THE DESERT

Scriptures to Pray for Your Future Husband

Throughout this book we've provided you with character qualities to pray that God will instill in your future husband. If you're looking for more guidance on things to pray for, we've listed some of the most important qualities and our favorite scriptures to go with them. **There are fifty-two of them—one for each week of the year.** Don't stop with these. Use a special notebook or journal to make your own list. Be faithful about writing down other verses that whisper to you about the longings you have for your future husband—and yourself.

1. Pray your future husband will turn to God for salvation. Pray he will see God as his strength and his song.
    Surely God is my salvation; I will trust and not be afraid. The Lord, the Lord himself, is my strength and my defense; he has become my salvation. (Isaiah 12:2, NIV)

2. Pray God guides him in paths of righteousness, so God's name will be honored.
    He refreshes my soul. He guides me along the right paths for his name's sake. (Psalm 23:3, NIV)

3. Pray he will call to God for every need.
    But I've lost it. I'm wasted. God—quickly, quickly! Quick to my side, quick to my rescue! God, don't lose a minute. (Psalm 70:5, MSG)

4. Pray he will trust God and not be afraid. Pray God will be his defense.

   God, my strength, I am looking to you, because God is my defender. (Psalm 59:9, NCV)

5. Pray God's face will shine on him.

   The LORD bless you and keep you; the LORD make his face shine on you and be gracious to you; the LORD turn his face toward you and give you peace. (Numbers 6:24–26, NIV)

6. Pray he will submit to God.

   In all your ways submit to him, and he will make your paths straight. (Proverbs 3:6, NIV)

7. Pray he will have a heart tender toward God's instruction.

   I will praise the LORD, who counsels me; even at night my heart instructs me. (Psalm 16:7, NIV)

8. Pray he will run to the Lord as a strong tower.

   The name of the LORD is a fortified tower; the righteous run to it and are safe. (Proverbs 18:10, NIV)

9. Pray God will be his hiding place.

   You are my hiding place; you will protect me from trouble and surround me with songs of deliverance. (Psalm 32:7, NIV)

10. Pray he will enjoy God and seek God's pleasure above his own—and that God will give him the desires of his heart.

    Take delight in the LORD, and he will give you the desires of your heart. (Psalm 37:4, NIV)

11. Pray he will desire a suitable helper.

    The LORD God said, "It is not good for the man to be alone. I will make a helper suitable for him." (Genesis 2:18, NIV)

12. Pray he will come to God to be changed so that he will remain blameless.

    May God himself, the God of peace, sanctify you through and through. May your whole spirit, soul and body be kept blameless at the coming of our Lord Jesus Christ. (1 Thessalonians 5:23, NIV)

13. Pray he will see his own faults and be sympathetic to the faults of others.

    Why do you look at the speck of sawdust in your brother's eye and pay no attention to the plank in your own eye? (Matthew 7:3, NIV)

14. Pray he will run the race to win the prize.

    Do you not know that in a race all the runners run, but only one gets the prize? Run in such a way as to get the prize. Everyone who competes in the games goes into strict training. They do it to get a crown that will not last, but we do it to get a crown that will last forever. Therefore I do not run like someone running aimlessly; I do not fight like a boxer beating the air. No, I strike a blow to my body and make it my slave so that after I have preached to others, I myself will not be disqualified for the prize. (1 Corinthians 9:24–27, NIV)

15. Pray he will stand firm in God's will.

    He is always wrestling in prayer for you, that you may

*stand firm in all the will of God, mature and fully
assured.* (Colossians 4:12, NIV)

16. Pray he will know the hope to which God has called
him.

*I pray that the eyes of your heart may be enlightened in
order that you may know the hope to which he has called
you, the riches of his glorious inheritance in his holy
people, and his incomparably great power for us who
believe. That power is the same as the mighty strength.*
(Ephesians 1:18–19, NIV)

17. Pray he will be alert.

*With this in mind, be alert and always keep on praying
for all the Lord's people.* (Ephesians 6:18, NIV)

18. Pray he will learn to speak the truth from his heart.

*LORD, who may dwell in your sacred tent? Who may live
on your holy mountain? The one whose walk is blameless,
who does what is righteous, who speaks the truth from
their heart.* (Psalm 15:1–2, NIV)

19. Pray he will be content.

*I am not saying this because I am in need, for I have
learned to be content whatever the circumstances.*
(Philippians 4:11, NIV)

*But godliness with contentment is great gain. For we
brought nothing into the world, and we can take nothing
out of it. But if we have food and clothing, we will be
content with that.* (1 Timothy 6:6–8, NIV)

20. Pray he won't do things the world's way but rather
God's way.

*Do not conform to the pattern of this world, but be
transformed by the renewing of your mind. Then
you will be able to test and approve what God's will
is—his good, pleasing and perfect will.* (Romans
12:2, NIV)

21. Pray he keeps his thoughts obedient to Christ.
*We demolish arguments and every pretension that sets
itself up against the knowledge of God, and we take
captive every thought to make it obedient to Christ.*
(2 Corinthians 10:5, NIV)

22. Pray God's presence will make him strong and
courageous.
*Be strong and courageous. Do not be afraid or terrified
because of them, for the LORD your God goes with you; he
will never leave you nor forsake you.* (Deuteronomy
31:6, NIV)

23. Pray he will take all of his requests before God.
*Do not be anxious about anything, but in every situation,
by prayer and petition, with thanksgiving, present your
requests to God. And the peace of God, which transcends
all understanding, will guard your hearts and your minds
in Christ Jesus.* (Philippians 4:6–7, NIV)

24. Pray he will set his mind on things that are noble.
*Finally, brothers and sisters, whatever is true, whatever is
noble, whatever is right, whatever is pure, whatever is
lovely, whatever is admirable—if anything is excellent or
praiseworthy—think about such things. Whatever you
have learned or received or heard from me, or seen in*

me—put it into practice. And the God of peace will be with you. (Philippians 4:8–9, NIV)

25. Pray he will submit to God and resist the devil.

    Submit yourselves, then, to God. Resist the devil, and he will flee from you. (James 4:7, NIV)

26. Pray he will leave the ways of childhood behind as he grows and matures.

    When I was a child, I talked like a child, I thought like a child, I reasoned like a child. When I became a man, I put the ways of childhood behind me. (1 Corinthians 13:11, NIV)

    Until we all reach unity in the faith and in the knowledge of the Son of God and become mature, attaining to the whole measure of the fullness of Christ. (Ephesians 4:13, NIV)

27. Pray he will hope in the Lord.

    Those who hope in the LORD will renew their strength. They will soar on wings like eagles; they will run and not grow weary, they will walk and not be faint. (Isaiah 40:31, NIV)

28. Pray he will have spiritual power and will grasp Christ's love.

    For this reason I kneel before the Father, from whom every family in heaven and on earth derives its name. I pray that out of his glorious riches he may strengthen you with power through his Spirit in your inner being, so that Christ may dwell in your hearts through faith. And I pray that you, being rooted and established in love, may have power, together with all the Lord's holy people, to grasp how wide and long and high and deep is the love of Christ, and to know this love that surpasses knowledge— that you may be filled to the measure of all the fullness of God. (Ephesians 3:14–19, NIV)

29. Pray he will surround himself with wise friends.
    Walk with the wise and become wise, for a companion of fools suffers harm. (Proverbs 13:20, NIV)

30. Pray for his humility.
    Do not think of yourself more highly than you ought, but rather think of yourself with sober judgment, in accordance with the faith God has distributed to each of you. (Romans 12:3, NIV)

31. Pray he will be open to instruction.
    Hold on to instruction, do not let it go; guard it well, for it is your life. (Proverbs 4:13, NIV)

32. Pray he learns to love as God desires him to.
    Love is patient, love is kind. It does not envy, it does not boast, it is not proud. It does not dishonor others, it is not self-seeking, it is not easily angered, it keeps no record of wrongs. Love does not delight in evil but rejoices with the truth. It always protects, always trusts, always hopes, always perseveres. (1 Corinthians 13:4–7, NIV)

33. Pray he cares for others and is generous.
    If it is to encourage, then give encouragement; if it is giving, then give generously; if it is to lead, do it diligently; if it is to show mercy, do it cheerfully. (Romans 12:8, NIV)

34. Pray he will not grow weary in doing good.

    Let us not become weary in doing good, for at the proper time we will reap a harvest if we do not give up. (Galatians 6:9, NIV)

35. Pray he will grow in the fruit of the Spirit.

    But the fruit of the Spirit is love, joy, peace, forbearance, kindness, goodness, faithfulness, gentleness and self-control. Against such things there is no law. (Galatians 5:22–23, NIV)

36. Pray he will bear fruit and become a disciple of Jesus.

    This is to my Father's glory, that you bear much fruit, showing yourselves to be my disciples. (John 15:8, NIV)

37. Pray his character will build so he will be effective and productive.

    For this very reason, make every effort to add to your faith goodness; and to goodness, knowledge; and to knowledge, self-control; and to self-control, perseverance; and to perseverance, godliness; and to godliness, mutual affection; and to mutual affection, love. For if you possess these qualities in increasing measure, they will keep you from being ineffective and unproductive in your knowledge of our Lord Jesus Christ. (2 Peter 1:5–8, NIV)

38. Pray God will guard his course.

    For he guards the course of the just and protects the way of his faithful ones. (Proverbs 2:8, NIV)

39. Pray he will live wisely.

    Be very careful, then, how you live—not as unwise but as wise. (Ephesians 5:15, NIV)

40. Pray he will be a man of integrity.

   The integrity of the upright guides them. (Proverbs 11:3
   NIV)

41. Pray he will have God's song in his mouth.

   *He put a new song in my mouth, a hymn of praise to our
   God. Many will see and fear the LORD and put their trust
   in him.* (Psalm 40:3, NIV)

42. Pray he will fear the Lord and praise Him.

   *The fear of the LORD is the beginning of wisdom; all who
   follow his precepts have good understanding. To him
   belongs eternal praise.* (Psalm 111:10, NIV)

43. Pray he will seek God first.

   *But seek first his kingdom and his righteousness, and all
   these things will be given to you as well.* (Matthew 6:33,
   NIV)

44. Pray he will turn to God to help him live the godly life
   he desires.

   *We plan the way we want to live, but only GOD makes us
   able to live it.* (Proverbs 16:9, MSG)

45. Pray he will be strong and walk as God requires.

   *So be strong, act like a man, and observe what the LORD
   your God requires: Walk in obedience to him, and keep his
   decrees and commands, his laws and regulations, as written
   in the Law of Moses. Do this so that you may prosper in all
   you do and wherever you go.* (1 Kings 2:2–3, NIV)

46. Pray he'll allow the Lord to direct his steps.

   *The LORD directs the steps of the godly. He delights in
   every detail of their lives.* (Psalm 37:23, NLT)

47. Pray he'll conquer evil by doing good.

Don't let evil conquer you, but conquer evil by doing good. (Romans 12:21, NLT)

48. Pray he'll live a self-controlled life that is a result of his salvation.

For the grace of God has appeared that offers salvation to all people. It teaches us to say "No" to ungodliness and worldly passions, and to live self-controlled, upright and godly lives in this present age. (Titus 2:11–12, NIV)

49. Pray he doesn't walk, stand, or sit with ungodly friends.

Blessed is the one who does not walk in step with the wicked or stand in the way that sinners take or sit in the company of mockers, but whose delight is in the law of the LORD, and who meditates on his law day and night. (Psalm 1:1–2, NIV)

50. Pray he will grow and flourish because of his trust in the Lord.

But blessed is the one who trusts in the LORD, whose confidence is in him. They will be like a tree planted by the water that sends out its roots by the stream. It does not fear when heat comes; its leaves are always green. It has no worries in a year of drought and never fails to bear fruit. (Jeremiah 17:7–8, NIV)

51. Pray he will not be puffed up but will live by faithfulness.

See, the enemy is puffed up; his desires are not upright— but the righteous person will live by his faithfulness. (Habakkuk 2:4, NIV)

52. Pray the Lord will keep him from all harm.

The LORD will keep you from all harm—he will watch over your life; the LORD will watch over your coming and going both now and forevermore. (Psalm 121:7–8, NIV)

Acknowledgments

The first person we must thank is Hannah. We are so grateful to God and to your mom that at the last minute you ended up coming to dinner with us in Denver two years ago. If it hadn't been for your enthusiasm over this project and your persistence in talking to the right people, this book might still be unpublished. We are also very grateful to all the women who gave us permission to share their stories of how they prayed and how God answered. Your testimonies shine like stars in this book. Thank you, Rachel and Josiah, for sharing your poetic thoughts on waiting and trusting God for just the right person to share your life with. Oh, how He answered! Many thanks go to our wonderful editor, Alice Crider, for believing in this project from the beginning and encouraging us every step of the way. Janet Grant, our phenomenal agent, we could never have done this without you. Your lovely fingerprints are on every page. You saw what this book could be and somehow managed to keep two creative novelists on track to write a nonfiction book. Above all we want to thank our Heavenly Father for answering our prayers and giving both of us God-Lover husbands.

CAN'T GET ENOUGH OF ROBIN JONES GUNN?

Christy Miller Collection, Volume 1 (Books 1-3)
Christy Miller Collection, Volume 2 (Books 4-6)
Christy Miller Collection, Volume 3 (Books 7-9)
Christy Miller Collection, Volume 4 (Books 10-12)

Sierra Jensen Collection, Volume 1 (Books 1-3)
Sierra Jensen Collection, Volume 2 (Books 4-6)
Sierra Jensen Collection, Volume 3 (Books 7-9)
Sierra Jensen Collection, Volume 4 (Books 10-12)

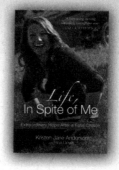

To learn more about
ROBIN JONES GUNN
visit www.robingunn.com

Follow Robin!

www.facebook.com/robin.jones.gunn

www.twitter.com/robingunn

http://shop.robingunn.com

You can find out more about
TRICIA GOYER
and her books at www.triciagoyer.com

Tricia also wrote two other books for teens: *My Life, Unscripted: Who's Writing Your Life* (Thomas Nelson) and *Life Interrupted: The Scoop On Being a Young Mom* (Zondervan).

Follow Tricia!

www.facebook.com/tricia.goyer

www.twitter.com/triciagoyer

http://triciagoyer.blogspot.com